Improving Transition Planning for Young People with Special Educational Needs

Lesley Dee

Open University Press

KH

Open University Press
McGraw-Hill Education
McGraw-Hill House
Shoppenhangers Road
Maidenhead
Berkshire
England
SL6 2QL

email: enquiries@openup.co.uk
world wide web: www.openup.co.uk

and Two Penn Plaza, New York, NY 10121-2289, USA

First published 2006

A catalogue record of this book is available from the British Library

ISBN 10: 0335 216 269 (pb) 0335 216293 (hb)
IISBN 13: 9780335216260 (pb) 9780335216291 (hb)

Library of Congress Cataloging-in-Publication Data
CIP data applied for

Typeset by YHT Ltd
Printed in Poland by OZGraf S.A.
www.polskabook.pl

9/18/06

Improving Transition Planning for Young People with Special Educational Needs

Dedication

To my father and mother.

Contents

List of tables and figures

Acknowledgements

I would like to express my thanks to all those who have supported me in writing this book. To Sue Hallam who suggested the idea in the first place and then to Jenny Evans, Helen Hayhoe, Liz Maudslay and Margaret Palmer who all acted as the best critical friends I could wish for. I am also indebted to the young people and their families who allowed me to tell their stories and to all the teachers and other professionals who made time to see me and became as interested and committed to the project as I was.

1 Introduction

1.1 Why this book

This book is about how decisions are reached about the post-school destinations of young people described as having special educational needs. I
became interested several years ago when I noticed that young people with
very similar needs from two different schools in the same local authority
followed very different routes when they reached the age of 16. In one
instance most stayed on at school while in the other the majority left and
went to the local college. Why was this? What influenced these decisions?
And more importantly who was making the decisions and why?

The research on which the book is based lasted three years during which I
followed the stories of 12 young people as they prepared to leave school. I
wanted to discover how decisions were taken about what they would do and
where they would go as well as the influences on those decisions. But I also
wanted to know what could be done to improve the process not just at the
point of leaving school but throughout the transition from school to adult
life. As with all research the situation has changed since the information was
collected and some things may well have improved. Despite this, many issues
and problems remain and my hope is that this book will contribute to the on-
going debate about how best to improve planning for transition as well as
providing some ideas for practitioners who want to make a difference.

Over the last 25 years there have been a number of enquiries into the
post-school destinations of young adults with learning difficulties and/or
disabilities in the UK (Anderson and Clarke 1982; Walker 1982; Clarke and
Hirst 1989; Riddell et al. 1993; Armstrong and Davies 1995; Hornby and Kidd
2001). This research has confirmed what is generally held to be the case that

- disabled people including those with learning difficulties are grossly
  disadvantaged in the labour market;
- the demands of the labour market are changing; and
- having a job does not necessarily guarantee a good quality of life.

In recent years policy makers have turned their attention to the quality of
support that is available to young people with special educational needs and
their families during the transition from school. There has been a plethora of
policy initiatives, discussed in more detail in Chapter 2. There remains

however a gap between policy and practice and one of the aims of this book is to support practitioners in improving the quality of transition planning processes and the support that it is offered to young people.

The aims of this book are therefore to:

- provide insights into the experiences and perspectives of young people, their parents or carers and the professionals who support them during the transition period;
- explore influences on the decision-making processes and the involvement of young people and their parents or carers;
- suggest practical ways in which young people and their families and carers can be supported during the transition to adulthood.

1.2 The structure of the book

In this first Chapter, I introduce the main ideas that are explored throughout the rest of the book as well as the young people on whose stories the book is based. Chapter 2 summarizes the current legislative and policy context. Since the original research on which this book is based was carried out there have been a number of important policy developments. But since 1997 when the Labour government came to power the general thrust of social policy has remained the same as have many of the practical difficulties. The core of the book, Chapters 3, 4, 5 and 6, describes the experiences of the young people as they prepare to leave school, beginning with an analysis of the kind of decision-making processes in which they were involved. The young people were supported and influenced by family members or carers as well as a range of professionals. The sometimes conflicting or different perspectives of each of these three groups of people (the young people, their families or carers and the professionals) are then explored in some detail. The chapters describe the unfolding events over the course of the three years of the study as the young people were beginning to leave school. While the events themselves may be similar, such as a particular meeting or encounter, how the key players understood these events was often very different. The final chapter explores the implications of these different perspectives for the curriculum and the support that is provided.

At the end of each chapter there is a section called 'Improving transition planning' where you will find suggested staff development activities and ideas for improving transition planning. These suggestions are likely to be most effective when used by interdisciplinary teams wishing to improve their current practice and who are drawn from schools, colleges, Connexions Services and other organizations that are concerned with the transition of young people with a range of special educational needs.

1.3 Who are the young people?

The young people who are the focus of this study have all been identified by the school system as having special educational needs. Each young person required adaptations to enable them to access the curriculum arising from their particular impairments. The *Code of Practice* (DfES 2001) identifies the following areas of need:

- Communication and interaction
- Cognition and learning
- Behaviour, emotional and social development
- Sensory and/or physical development

The extent to which these difficulties are internal to the individual, as opposed to resulting from factors within the environment, is an on-going debate. However, most commentators now accept that special educational needs are the result of interactions between individual characteristics and the environment. While many difficulties in learning can present permanently disabling barriers they can also be reduced or even removed through changing or modifying factors within the learner's environment.

Once a young person leaves school it is important to recognize that labels applied in one context may have very little meaning or relevance in another. For instance some young people who experienced difficulties in learning at school are absorbed into the labour market with relative ease. If they go on to further education or training, statements of special educational needs no longer apply as legal documents. Some young people may lose their label altogether while others are referred to as having 'learning difficulties and/or disabilities' or 'additional support needs'. But these catch-all phrases have become increasingly unhelpful in describing the wide range of learners that the term encompasses. While labels can help in attracting additional funding and support, they often provide few clues about learning needs and at worst may invite low expectations or even stigma and suspicion.

1.4 What is transition?

The term transition has become largely synonymous with the period of leaving school. Yet as Cooley and Moeschler (1993) point out we experience many transitions throughout our lives which are shared by most members of society, for example, getting married and moving jobs, while others are fundamental to life itself, for example, birth, puberty and death. As well as the anticipation and excitement brought about by these periods of change and flux they can also generate anxiety, uncertainty and stress.

I want to begin this discussion on the nature of school to post-school transitions with the definition provided by McGinty and Fish in 1992:

> ... a phase or period of time between the teens and twenties which is broken up educationally and administratively. During the phase there are changes of responsibility from child to adult services, from school to further and higher education and from childhood dependence to adult responsibility ... a process by which the individual grows through adolescence to adulthood and achieves the balanced state of dependence and independence which a particular community expects of its adult members.
>
> (1992: 6)

The value of this particular definition lies in the distinction that McGinty and Fish draw between the administrative and legislative procedures that govern this period for young disabled people including those with learning difficulties and the processes that the young person experiences and how these are understood. The first phase of the transition process is governed by the guidance set out in the 2001 *Code of Practice* (DfES), starting when the young person is in Year 9 (aged 13+) and extending through to age 19 or whenever they leave school. Schools, working in collaboration with the Connexions Service and other statutory agencies, have a duty to prepare a transition plan for all young people with statements of special educational needs, beginning in Year 9 and reviewed annually until the student leaves school. The young people and their parents must be involved in this process. Changes of responsibility for education can shift from schools to further education, for health and care from child to adult services. If the young person goes on to further education and/or training the requirement to hold a transition plan review no longer applies.

A distinguishing feature of the transition process for disabled young people as opposed to their non-disabled peers, is the often very public and bureaucratic nature of the decision-making processes. At a private level the processes are similar for everyone, disabled and non-disabled alike. In their study of young people in the process of leaving school Ball et al. describe them as, 'full of doubts and indecisions, changes of mind, vague possibilities' (2000: 15). But for young people with disabilities the process of leaving school and deciding what to do next is also one that is conducted largely in public often involving a large number of different agencies. Governed by a series of administrative procedures, decisions are, on the face of it, often made and recorded at formal meetings. It is therefore both a public and a private process with the public and bureaucratic aspects of the process sometimes dominating the essentially very ordinary personal confusion and uncertainty.

McGinty and Fish also refer to the *process* of transition. I want to explore the process of transition from three different but complementary perspectives described as phase-related, agency-related and time-related.

Phase-related model of transition

The phase-related model of transition regards the transition to adulthood as one of a number of stages through which individuals pass during their lifetime (Levinson 1998). This approach was adopted by the Centre for Educational Research and Innovation (CERI) (1986) which defines the final years of secondary education as the first part of 'a continuous journey that starts well before pupils leave school and does not end when they first enter work' (p. 42). Young people grow through the period of adolescence to adulthood. Adulthood means having

- paid employment;
- personal autonomy with legal and civil rights;
- friendships and social activities; and
- family roles and responsibilities.

However disabled adults and young people may be prevented from being recognized as adolescents and being accorded adult status by a range of factors including the negative attitudes and assumptions of others, limited access to new opportunities and experiences, a lack of information and shifts in a labour market that is demanding an increasingly skilled workforce. The guidance in the *Code of Practice* (DfES 2001) on transition planning reflects this phase-related model beginning when the young person is in Year 9 and extending up to the point at which the young person leaves school. Young people are encouraged with the support of their families or carers and professionals to identify goals and targets for their adult lives, anticipating that by their early 20s the young person will have achieved a relatively settled adulthood.

Agency-related model of transition

The second set of ideas related to transition reflects the degree of agency or control that an individual has in determining the course of their lives. In the past sociologists maintained that post-school destinations were largely determined by class, gender and ethnicity rather than by personal choice (Roberts 1971; Willis 1977). More recently social theorists have concluded that individuals are beginning to have more freedom to challenge the taken for granted assumptions of society and make their own decisions and choices about who they are and who they want to become but that family, socioeconomic status, gender and ethnicity continue to maintain a strong influence (Gambetta 1987; Hodkinson et al. 1996; Foskett and Hesketh 1997; Ball et al. 2000). But while there is evidence of increased mobility within mainstream society, however slight, those on the margins including those with a range of learning difficulties and disabilities continue to have very little control over the direction of their lives. Hughes et al. (2005) suggest that most mainstream debates about the structure of society overlook those with disabilities and that many barriers remain in place. Three studies exemplify this point. Heslop et al. (2002) examined the experiences of young people with a range of learning difficulties during the school leaving period. Morris (1999) looked at the lives of a group of young people with learning difficulties or physical and sensory impairments after they had left school while Dyson et al. (2002) explored the experiences of a group of 'disadvantaged' rather than disabled special school leavers. All found that despite the fact that the young people had ideas of their own they were not actively involved in exploring who they wanted to become and determining the kind of lives they wanted to lead.

Time-related model of transition

The time-related model integrates ideas drawn from several different schools of thought: biology, social–psychology and sociology. As Price and Patton (2003) point out, those working in education increasingly look beyond ideas drawn from a single school of thought but instead combine ideas from several disciplines, using what works best. Taking time as the starting point for thinking about the transition from school to adult life also helps to place the transition from school in broader ideas about adult development. Merriam (1999) uses time as a comprehensive and all encompassing idea to understand more about the nature of adult learning and development. By locating the school leaving stage in theories of adult learning and development adolescent transitions are seen as a single point in the process of lifelong development. Using time-related ideas helps to take the long view when thinking about transition and young people with special educational needs and forces us to look beyond the school gate. Merriam identifies three dimensions of time that influence the development of adults: historical, life and social time.

- *Historical time*: This describes the impact of long-term social, economic and legislative changes on the lives of individuals. Changes
  include shifts in the economy, the nature of work and their effects on
  the labour market; improved communication brought about by
  advances in technology; scientific and medical advances; changes in
  legislation. The impact of these changes on the lives of people with
  learning difficulties and/or disabilities are both positive and negative.
  Positive outcomes include higher survival rates among babies born

with complex medical conditions, and improvements in augmentative communication aids for those with communication and interaction needs. On the negative side the demands of the labour market for increasingly flexible and highly skilled workers excludes those who might have obtained work in the past while continuing to exclude others.

- *Life time*: This is another way of describing predictable, age-related changes. These include biological and functional changes linked to age such as learning to walk and talk, entering puberty, having children, ageing and so forth. Rates of development vary across the population. Because the development of young people with special educational needs may be delayed physically and/or intellectually other people may fail to see them as an adolescent with all the associated feelings, wants and needs.

- *Social time*: The third dimension, social time, describes the rights, duties, responsibilities and expectations that are conferred on individuals at different stages of their life. Society creates norms that are associated with different phases of our lives. Griffiths (1994), for example, describes the gradual shift of responsibilities that occurs during adolescence as the young person moves from being a dependent child to gradually assuming more responsibility for themselves and subsequently others.

But societies' expectations are not fixed, they change over time. For instance the expectations the Elizabethan and Victorians had of their young people are very different from those of the twenty-first century. Young people now remain in education and training and live at home much longer than they did even 50 years ago. Equally expectations vary between cultures – while Western society emphasizes the importance of the freedom to make choices and develop autonomy, Browder et al. (2001) and Greenfield et al. (2003) point out that these qualities are not valued nearly as much by other societies. Different cultures emphasize different degrees of autonomy and relatedness which vary not only between cultures but between ethnic minorities within the same society.

Societies develop rituals and rites of passage to mark the passing of time that help to give a sense of direction and purpose to life. These rituals may also relieve the stress and anxiety associated with some transitions. Markers associated with young people's coming of age vary between cultures and between groups and include celebrations, displays of physical courage, religious ceremonies and so forth. As young people with special educational needs approach the school leaving stage, many may not have participated in the familiar rituals and activities associated with adolescence, for example, gaining qualifications, having a first boyfriend or girlfriend, learning to drive.

This reinforces for parents what their child cannot do, as well as exacerbating fears that parents may have for the future thereby increasing their levels of stress and anxiety. While certain life events are expected and can be planned for, such as leaving school, having a baby or retiring, others are unexpected. Mitchell in her study of special school leavers commented, 'Events can and do just occur ... there is always an element of chance' (1999: 763). Sometimes these unexpected events confirm previously held ideas and opinions or they can transform them, causing us to change our minds. For example, we might have been contemplating changing jobs over several months or even years. A chance conversation may lead to a new job (or cause us to stay where we are!). While some chance events may turn out to be fortuitous other unplanned events can be more stressful (falling ill, being made redundant, giving birth to a disabled child) and in these instances greater personal as well as external resources are required. Finally, life events may be self-initiated, such as deciding to move house or get married or they may be externally initiated, such as being expelled from school or sacked from work. People with learning difficulties, particularly those with complex needs, are least likely to be afforded control over what happens in their lives.

To conclude, the concept of transition is more than just an administrative point in time. The transition process implies change and uncertainty which can lead to feelings of anxiety and loss of control as well as excitement and challenge. The transition to adulthood implies changes in status, both in how we see ourselves as well as in how others see us, changes that may be denied to young people with learning difficulties and/or disabilities. These ideas and their implications for families and young people are explored throughout the rest of this book. Here is a summary of the arguments that I explore.

- Making decisions during adolescence is messy, complex and difficult for disabled and non-disabled young people alike.
- A distinguishing feature of the decision-making process for young disabled people is its public and often bureaucratic nature.
- Decisions evolve slowly and over time and people may change their minds.
- Effective support for young people with disabilities and learning difficulties in transition involves recognizing that their experiences will be both the same as and different from those of their non-disabled peers.
- Defining young people first and foremost by their disability or learning difficulty gets in the way of acknowledging their aspirations, choices and dilemmas.
- Understanding other people's perspectives and 'walking in their shoes' can help in negotiating decisions.

- Everyone needs a voice and to be heard equally within the decision-making processes.
- Transition planning is best supported by working with the grain of the decision-making processes and enhancing the personal and external resources of young people and their families.
- The 14–25 curriculum in schools and colleges should become more transition focused.

Before exploring these ideas in more detail however I want to recap what is known about where young people go when they leave school.

1.5 Transition to what?

When young people dream about the future they think about the whole of their lives: where they'll go, what they'll do, where they'll live and who they'll become. Yet policy and practice tends to segment people's lives and dwell on education, training or employment, neglecting, for example, their housing needs or opportunities for making friends or developing new interests. Of course these are all interdependent. Living in a decent house, having family and friends and leading a full and active life is generally dependent on having relevant education and training, a good job and sufficient income. In this section I outline what we know about the lives of young people with special educational needs beyond the statutory school leaving age.

The number of young people in general remaining in further education and training beyond 16 has risen to around 75 percent over the last 25 years (OECD 2004). Mirroring this trend the number of young people with a range of learning difficulties participating in further education and training has also increased. The reasons underlying these increases are complex and are linked to the kind of historical changes that I have already described, including demands in the labour market for a more highly skilled workforce. The effect of these changes on young people with special educational needs has been particularly noticeable. In 1982 Walker found that employment rates among 18-year-olds with and without learning difficulties or disabilities were broadly similar (66 percent). However while the remainder without disabilities were in some form of education or training those with learning difficulties or disabilities were at home or attending social services day centres. Twenty-five years on the DfES's (Dewson et al. 2004) longitudinal survey of post-school destinations for young people with special educational needs found that nearly half of the 17- and 18-year-olds were still at school or college while 28 percent were in employment. It is always difficult to compare studies of this nature because of differences in how target groups are defined and the nature of the sampling strategies. Despite these caveats, figures from the two studies show the rise in the number of learners with special educational needs now remaining in further education and training beyond 16. Yet critics argue that many young people move from one education and training programme to another not as a means of progression to employment but simply because there is nothing else for them to do (Riddell et al. 2001; Armstrong 2003). Meanwhile inspections have challenged the quality of much of this provision (Ofsted 2004a, b; ALI 2004).

Having completed their training chances of employment are not good. A recent report from the Cabinet Office (2005) concluded,

> At the age of 26 disabled people without learning difficulties are more likely than non-disabled people to have no qualifications, to feel that they have not acquired useful skills, not in education employment or training [sic] and if they are in employment to be in unskilled work.
>
> (p. 149)

Some question the emphasis given to employment as the main marker of adulthood for people with disabilities. Yet in 1994 CERI asserted that open paid employment was the only satisfactory outcome for the transition phase, however long that lasts, since it is only through this route that disabled people can achieve a satisfactory quality of life. Other studies confirm the interdependence of access to employment and quality of life. A report from the European Agency for Development in Special Needs Education notes, '"A good life for all" as well as a "good job for all" are the ultimate goals of a successful overall transition process' (2002: 10).

As adults many of those with disabilities and learning difficulties are eligible for statutory support but they may find themselves socially isolated and/or in some form of specialist provision. The increase in employment schemes such as New Deal for the Disabled or Access to Work are more focused on adults returning to work rather than on young people trying to enter the employment market. So the situation remains that for many young people with special educational needs the transition period is characterized by time spent on inappropriate further education courses or government sponsored training schemes interspersed with increasingly longer spells of unemployment. Alternatively the modernization of day services, the closure of day centres and the introduction of community-based services has presented new kinds of freedoms as well as constraints for some young people with learning difficulties once they leave post-school education and training. These person-centred initiatives mean that clear available options are less evident and individuals are dependent on others to interpret their wishes for them.

What about the rest of their lives? Despite the growth of supported and independent living schemes, a survey conducted in 2003 showed that 40 percent of disabled young people aged 16–24 were living in unsuitable accommodation (ODPM 2003). They are much less likely than their non-disabled counterparts to use public transport, travelling a third less often. This means that they are more likely to be housebound and have fewer opportunities to build social networks, develop friendships and form intimate relationships. This in turn can lead to loneliness, social isolation and depression. As the Cabinet Office report concludes 'Poor outcomes are both a cause and a consequence of disability' (2005: 15). Having a low income, poor housing and a poor quality of life can lead to disadvantage and disability while having a disability can lead to disadvantage. What can be done to break into this cycle of disadvantage and social exclusion? Part of the answer lies in improving the quality of transition planning including strengthening the pathways between school and post-school education and training as well as child and adult services (Cabinet Office 2005).

Having set the scene for this study of transition and introduced some of the ideas that I intend to explore throughout the book, I turn now to the study itself and the young people and their families whose lives I followed over the course of three years as they prepared to leave school.

1.6 The young people

In all 12 young people and their parents or carers were involved in the study. There was a total of seven boys and five girls, four of whom came from ethnic minorities. One lived in a foster home, two came from single-parent families, while the rest lived with their birth families. In terms of school placement, three attended mainstream schools and nine were from special schools, with four students being partially or entirely residential. The intention in selecting the sample of pupils was to include, as far as possible, a range of areas of need reflecting the heterogeneity of young people with special educational needs, including those with and without statements, i.e., cognition and learning difficulties; sensory and physical impairments; emotional and behavioural difficulties; and communication and interaction difficulties. I also attempted to take account of race, gender, and social and economic status in deciding who to include in the study.

To ensure that no single factor influenced the transition process unduly two contrasting local authorities were selected: one an Outer-London borough where almost half its population comes from ethnic minorities and the other a shire county with less than 4 percent from ethnic minorities. The London borough was ranked as one of the most deprived boroughs in the country with 8.1 percent unemployed, whereas the shire county enjoyed a buoyant local economy with an unemployment rate of around 1.2 percent.

Data were collected over three years through a combination of interviews, observation, questionnaires administered over the telephone and a field log. At least one annual review and transition planning meeting for each casestudy pupil was observed followed by a telephone interview with parents and a questionnaire to professionals designed to explore the perceived usefulness of the meetings.

The following brief descriptions are intended to provide the reader with an initial introduction to the young people and their families. Each has been given a pseudonym and they are listed in alphabetical order. The young people are described as they were when I first met them along with a postscript describing what they were doing by the end of the research. As well as these pen portraits, brief profiles of the young people, their parents and carers can also be found in the Appendix.

Andrew Bailey

Andrew was profoundly deaf and relied mainly on sign language for communication. He was 15 years old when I first met him. He had a pleasant open face with an often serious expression when he was concentrating. His family lived in a small country town where his father worked as an electrician. His mother did not work outside the home. Andrew had one older brother who was still at school. Since he was 8 Andrew had been a weekly boarder at a school for deaf and hearing impaired pupils in a neighbouring county. He wanted to become an electrician like his father although he also harboured a secret desire to become a famous film star.

By the end of the study, Andrew was attending a residential specialist college for the deaf while studying engineering at a local sector college.

Costas Demetrios

Costas was 15 and lived at home with his parents, an older brother and a younger sister. Both his parents had emigrated from Cyprus to England before they were married. Now his father worked as a transport manager with the Post Office while his mother had a hairdressing business which she ran from home. For the last four years Costas had attended a local all-age special school for children with moderate learning difficulties, having previously attended a variety of schools. One morning a week he went to the local comprehensive where he was studying GCSE art. He wanted a girlfriend.

Costas was still at school by the end of the study but was likely to go on to a course at the local college.

David Francis

David was 14 years old and a day pupil at the same schools as Andrew. A tall good-looking boy, he was profoundly deaf. He lived at home with his father who had been a builder but then took a degree at the local university. His father was separated from his mother who worked as a communicator. David had one older brother at college. His parents had moved to this particular authority because they wanted David to remain in special education rather than attend a local comprehensive, as was the policy of their previous local authority. David wanted to work with animals when he left school.

When David left school he went to a residential specialist college for the deaf.

Gavin Stone

Gavin, 14, was Afro-Caribbean. He lived with a foster mother who worked as a prison officer. His foster father, who was retired, was away in the West Indies. According to his foster mother, Gavin had been taken into care along with his brothers and sisters when he was 5. He was however still in touch with his mother whom he visited once a month. He attended a local comprehensive school and had been identified as having emotional and behavioural difficulties. He had a statement of special educational needs and received support from a member of the local education authority's behaviour support service. His ambition was to work with animals, to get married and to have a dog and a snake as pets.

I lost contact with Gavin, but he was reported to be living in a squat with Somali asylum seekers after leaving school.

James Simpson

James, 15, who used a wheelchair, had been at the same school since he was two and a half years of age. He envisaged staying at school for one or two more years. His family home was some 15 miles away from the school and so he boarded at school two nights a week. He was the middle child of three sons. His mother was a part-time nursery teacher and his father, a plumber. James saw himself as a very active and sociable person and his ambition had originally been to become a policeman, although now he felt that this was unlikely. Instead he was unclear about what he wanted to do, although as far as his future lifestyle was concerned he wanted to live on his own in a flat.

James went on to do a computer course at a residential specialist college for physically disabled students.

Kim Doyle

Kim, 16, lived at home with her parents and her younger twin sister and brother. She had moderate learning difficulties and communication difficulties. After spending several years in the building trade her father had become a storeman at a local supermarket. Kim attended a local special school for pupils with moderate learning difficulties where she had been since she was 5 years of age. Her parents were very concerned about her travelling independently. Kim wanted to work with computers.

By the end of the study, Kim was about to join a pre-entry level course at her local college of further education.

Kylie Long

Kylie was 14 years of age when we first met. She was small and rather shy, giving the impression of frailty. Her mother was a single parent and, as the eldest child, Kylie had to take a lot of responsibility for caring for her three younger brothers. After their parents' separation the family had been homeless and lived in a women's refuge but they had now moved to a council house. Because of family circumstances Kylie had changed schools quite frequently, although she had been at her current comprehensive school for two years. She had a statement of special educational needs having been assessed as having moderate learning difficulties. In the long run she wanted either to work with computers or look after children. She expected to go on living at home when she left school but wanted eventually to find a place of her own.

Kylie dropped out of school and after failing to keep a work experience placement remained at home.

Malcolm Lewis

Malcolm, 15, attended the same school for children with moderate learning difficulties as Kim and Costas. A tall, thin boy with a pronounced stammer he lived with his parents on a large run-down council estate in London. He had a younger brother as well as an older sister and brother who were both married. His father was unemployed and agoraphobic. The family was hoping to be rehoused – the house was damp and infested with rats. Malcolm enjoyed helping out at a family business which rented out furniture. He had a bad relationship with his younger brother who teased him, and he suffered from severe bouts of uncontrollable anger. When he left school he wanted to live alone in a 'big house in Enfield with a cat and a dog'. He also wanted to work as a deliveryman in his uncle's firm but was concerned that his inability to read maps might prevent him from doing so.

Malcolm dropped out of school in Year 12 and began doing a little work in his uncle's firm. His parents were sceptical that he would sustain this.

Maria Constandis

Maria was 17 and had Rhett's Syndrome. Recently she had begun to communicate through eye pointing. She lived for two weeks at a time in a private care home paid for by social services and then one week at home with her parents and younger brother. Her mother taught at a local college of further education. Maria attended a school for children with severe learning difficulties. She seemed to get great pleasure from music and dancing (she clapped and rocked excitedly when she saw a video of herself playing a drum) but disliked her regular sessions of physiotherapy. Her mother expected that Maria would go to a residential placement when she left school since she was highly sceptical about the quality of local provision.

By the end of the study, Maria was attending a residential care home for young women with Rhett's Syndrome.

Nasreen Hussein

Nasreen was aged 15 and a day pupil at a special school for blind and partially sighted pupils. She was taking nine GCSEs some of which she studied for at a local comprehensive school. She lived with her parents, her grandfather, her younger brother and two older sisters who were both at college. Her brother was also blind and went to the same school as Nasreen. She was due to leave school at the end of the year and her ambition was to go to Downshire College, a residential specialist college for the blind. In the longer term, her ambition was to become a clinical psychologist and she was considering applications to the Universities of London, Oxford and Cambridge.

Due to unforeseen medical problems, Nasreen had to stay on at her residential specialist college for a third year.

Sandra Harding

Sandra, 15, lived with her parents and older brother on a council estate in a town in the Home Counties. Her mother worked for an insurance company and her father was unemployed. Sandra had physical disabilities and learning difficulties and went to a school about 20 miles away for children with physical disabilities. She boarded one night a week, travelling back and forth on the school bus for the rest of the time. Her best friend lived nearby and they went out together on a regular basis to the nearby swimming pool and bowling alley. The whole family was involved in caring for Sandra, including grandparents, aunts and uncles. When asked about the future, Sandra said she would 'miss her Mum and Dad' implying that she thought she would have to go to a residential college. Her mother was adamant however that Sandra must attend a local college when she left school.

After a good deal of uncertainty, Sandra went on a part-time course at her local further education college.

Stuart Brown

Stuart, 14, lived on a council estate in one of the London overspill towns built in the 1950s. His mother worked as a midday meals supervisor in a local primary school and his father was a lorry driver. He was the middle child, with an older sister and a younger brother. Physically tall for his age Stuart tended to lumber along bumping into things in his path, a fact that seemed to land him in constant trouble at school. He attended a local comprehensive and although he did not have a statement he received support for his learning difficulties from the school's learning support team. According to the special educational needs coordinator (SENCO) he also had behaviour problems. At weekends he worked on the market for one of the stallholders but in the long-term he was considering carpentry, although he believed that his behaviour might prevent him from achieving this ambition.

On leaving school, Stuart got himself a warehouseman's job in a local firm and began learning to drive.

1.7 Conclusions

This chapter has introduced the ideas that are explored in more detail throughout the rest of the book. In it I have suggested that the transition from school is one of a number of transitions that we make throughout our life span and that our understanding of this phase in young people's lives is enhanced by exploring the historical, biological, psychological and socio-logical influences on adult development and their implications for young people with special educational needs and their future lives. I have also argued that while the experience of leaving school and making decisions about the future for young people with learning difficulties and/or disabilities is as complex and difficult as it is for all young people, there are also some important differences, not least the very public nature of the decision-making process. Finally I have introduced the young people whose stories help to illuminate some of these ideas. However before turning to an examination of how decisions were made about what would happen when the young people left school I begin by exploring the broader policy framework that governs the transition from school.

Improving transition planning

1   Think of a transition that you have made during the course of your life: it might be starting a new job, leaving home, getting married or becoming a parent. Make a note of how you felt. What factors helped you and what factors hindered you in coming to terms with the change in your life. What do these tell you about what needs to be in place to support young people during the transition process?

2   Divide into two groups. Each group should identify either
   •   the characteristics of adolescence; *or*
   •   the characteristics of adulthood.
   Now identify the barriers that prevent young people with disabilities from experiencing adolescence *or* disabled adults from being accorded adult status.
   What could you do in your setting to remove some of these barriers?

2   The policy framework

2.1 Introduction

The purpose of this chapter is to remind readers about the national policy context relating to transition, bearing in mind that the research for this book was carried out before some of the more recent initiatives described here were introduced. But as Thomas and Loxley point out, 'the introduction of new policy is not a discrete act, as it connects and interacts with existing policy and practice' (2001: 98). Recent policy initiatives in this area have been principally designed to improve the life chances of people with learning difficulties and disabilities. This is being achieved partly through widening opportunities and incentives to participate in education and training and partly through improving the quality of support that young people receive during their transition from school. An important policy thrust has been the government's attempts to improve joined up thinking across departments and between child and adult services. At present responsibility for young people shifts from schools to further or higher education between the ages of 16 and 19, from child to adult services in health at 16 and in social services at 18.

Common themes include:

- A recognition that leaving school is the initial stage of the transition process which can extend well into young adulthood.
- The need for some form of personalized plan which is regularly reviewed.
- The centrality of the aspirations and needs of the young people themselves in determining the provision with 'wrap around' services designed to support young people and their families.
- The full involvement of parents or carers.
- Planning that embraces young people's social and emotional needs as well as their educational and career development, and that requires coordinated responses at individual, local and strategic levels.
- Continuity between child and adult services.
- Inclusive opportunities leading to achievements and activities recognized as valuable by the individual and the wider society.

This review of English social policy from the early 1990s to the present includes legislative reforms designed to promote these seven aspirations. Recent policy development in relation to young people and adults with learning difficulties and/or disabilities has brought together and reinforced a number of useful and important strands aimed at improving the quality of transition planning and opening up post-school progression routes, emphasizing holistic, person-centred planning and interagency collaboration. By contrast many mainstream policy initiatives, if they do so at all, only consider the consequences for disabled people including those with learning difficulties in retrospect. Examples of retrospective policy making include the *Education Reform Act* (DES 1988) leading to the *Code of Practice on the Identification and Assessment of Special Educational Needs* (DfE 1994), the *Further and Higher Education Act* (DfE 1992) that led to the FEFC (1996) report, *Inclusive Learning*, and the introduction of the Connexions Service whose remit was subsequently changed to include disabled young people up to the age of 25.

There is always a gap between the aspirations of policy makers and their realization (Ball 1994; Ozga 2000; Thomas and Loxley 2001). This section also discusses briefly some of the emerging issues that have arisen in relation to each of these policies. Four aspects of policy are discussed: education, health and social care, employment and finally interdepartmental collaboration.

2.2 Education policy

The special educational needs *Code of Practice* was introduced by the 1993 Education Act (DfE 1993) and later revised following the 2001 Education (Special Educational Needs) (England) Regulations (DfES 2001). The section of the *Code* that deals with the transition from school states that every young person with a statement of special educational needs should have a transition plan from Year 9 that is reviewed annually. The young person and their parents or carers must be involved in the plan's formulation. The *Code* makes reference to other multi-agency legislation governing the work of the Connexions Service, Social Services, Further Education and the Health Service.

Responsibility for convening the Year 9 annual review and transition planning meeting rests with the school, although the LEA retains responsibility for overseeing the review process. The Connexions Service, discussed below, assumes a prominent role in providing support and information to the young person and their families and in enacting the plan. The guidance emphasizes the on-going nature of the transition planning process.

Despite good intentions, the effectiveness of these procedures in supporting school to post-school transitions has been questioned by Heslop et al. (2002) and Dewson et al. (2004). Heslop's survey of 280 young people with a learning disability aged 13–25 and their families, found that one-fifth did not have or did not know whether they had a transition plan while a quarter who had a plan had not been involved in devising it. The more extensive survey by Dewson et al. (2004) of nearly 2000 young people concluded that while written plans are important it is the strength of the pathways between pre- and post-16 service provision that is more important in supporting young people as they leave school.

1992 Further and Higher Education Act

This Act established the Further Education Funding Council (FEFC), taking colleges out of local education authority control and was the first piece of legislation that referred to further education colleges as having some responsibilities towards students with learning difficulties and/or disabilities. However the FEFC and the Training and Enterprise Council (TEC) were only required to 'have regard to' people with learning difficulties and/or dis- abilities, thereby allowing colleges and training schemes the freedom to select participants according to local demand. The Act recommended that colleges take account of information on transition plans in assessing students' requirements and any young person applying for residential college place- ment must first be assessed by a local sector college.

The enactment of this Act arguably strengthened post-school opportu- nities for some young people and adults with learning difficulties and/or disabilities (Macadam and Sutcliffe 1996). However the FEFC's review of the impact of the Act (FEFC, 1996) identified three groups of learners who con- tinued to be underrepresented in further and continuing education: those with profound and complex learning difficulties, people with mental health problems and young people with emotional and behavioural difficulties.

Learning and Skills Act 2000 and the Connexions Strategy

The subsequent Learning and Skills Act (DfEE 2000a) revised the funding arrangements for all post-16 education and training providers by creating two single funding bodies, the Learning and Skills Council (LSC) for England and the National Council for Education and Training for Wales. The LSC (Eng- land) oversees the funding arrangements carried out through 47 local coun- cils. The Act reiterated the councils' duties to have regard to the needs of people with learning difficulties and disabilities but also strengthened their duty to promote equality of opportunity between disabled and non-disabled people.

Opportunities for progression into further education courses for those with more complex needs were also strengthened by the Act. The Act abol- ished the expectation that to trigger funding all learners would have to demonstrate their capacity to move on to a course at a higher level (not that they would necessarily do so). Despite this amendment it is clear that the post-school education and training sectors will continue to require some means of regulating expenditure, possibly based on learner's progress against national targets, but quite how this is to be achieved continues to be debated. Overall the quality and range of post-school education and training remains open to the vagaries of local interpretations of national policies and funding arrangements.

Partly subject to the Learning and Skills Act, the Connexions Service in England was introduced in 2000 (DfEE 2000b) with full implementation from 2002 to support young people aged 13–19 during their transition from school, now extended to age 25 for some. At the heart of the Connexions Strategy are the personal advisers (PAs), an idea originally suggested by the 1978 Warnock Report. The central role of the Connexions Service personal adviser has been described as 'map maker, bridge builder, encouragement provider, truth teller and developer of educational, employment and social networks' (Grove and Giraud-Saunders 2003: 16). Personal advisers must be invited to and attend Year 9 reviews. They are responsible for implementing the transition plan and they are also responsible for coordinating the Section 140 assessments of the post-school education and training needs of every young person with a statement of special educational needs in their final year of schooling. The Connexions Service may continue to support some young people up to the age of 25.

Current evaluations are optimistic about the potential of Connexions to improve the prospects of young people with special educational needs (Grove and Giraud-Saunders 2003; Coles et al. 2004; Rowland-Crosby et al. 2004). There are four caveats. First, their research found that the role of the PA is not well understood by young people and other professionals. Second, many Connexions Service PAs have low expectations about what the young people with special educational needs can achieve. Third, there is a need for a better system of referrals and information sharing between agencies. Fourth, personal advisers require better support, supervision and management. At the time of writing the future of the Connexions Service remains uncertain.

Removing Barriers to Achievement (DfES 2004a)

This strategy document sets out the government's action plan for improving provision for children and young people with special educational needs. It includes a section on transition which reiterates the need to improve the quality of transition planning. Two main planks of activity are recommended:

- An expansion of education and training opportunities both pre- and post-16; and
- Improved access to open employment, including more supported

employment schemes and better information for professional and parents.

14–19 Education and Skills White Paper (DfES 2005)

The 14–19 White Paper on education and skills (DfES 2005) was produced in response to the report of the Working Group on 14–19 reform of the curriculum and qualifications framework (DfES 2004b). The reform group produced some radical proposals for an inclusive qualifications framework of diplomas that included young people working at pre-entry and entry levels. All learners were to follow a programme consisting of three components: core and main learning underpinned by a set of common skills, knowledge and attributes. The core consisted of functional mathematics, literacy and communication and ICT, extracurricular activities, an extended project and personal review and guidance. The main learning was made up of subjects chosen by the student according to their particular interests and aspirations. The government's response to these radical proposals was disappointing and can be loosely summed up as 'more of the same'. They suggest instead that with respect to students working below Level 2 there will be:

- More qualifications on offer
- A greater emphasis on extracurricular activities through the government's Extended Schools programme and Youth Matters policy (see below)
- A greater emphasis on literacy and numeracy (now termed functional skills)
- An expansion of the Entry to Employment programme to include Key Stage 4
- Better transition planning
- More employment opportunities

When the reform group's proposals were published many were optimistic that the education system was moving towards a much more inclusive qualifications framework that would have profound consequences for the transition curriculum for many young people with special educational needs. Instead this very conservative response maintained a remedial rather than entitlement view of the curriculum, a point to which I return in the final chapter.

2.3 Employment policy

The requirement of the 1993 Trade Union Reform Act that local training and enterprise councils (TECs) should have 'regard to' young people with learning difficulties and/or disabilities was superseded by the 2000 Learning and Skills Act that not only brought education and training together under the same funding umbrella but also required training providers to promote equality of opportunity between disabled and non-disabled people. An aim of these changes has been to improve progression between education, training and employment. The Employment Service has a responsibility to assist disabled people, including those with learning difficulties to find and keep work. Recent innovations include being able to replace wage subsidies to employers with payment to job coaches or mentors. The Entry to Employment (E2E) scheme provides extra time and support for those not able to access modern apprenticeships, and consists of training at Level 1 and below in literacy, language and numeracy, vocational skills and personal and social development. However there are concerns about the appropriateness of E2E for some learners with learning difficulties or disabilities. Other employment initiatives such as the New Deal for Disabled People are directed at those wishing to return to employment rather than young people leaving education. Reviews of supported employment schemes and work-based training have shown wide disparities in locally available relevant training at the right level (O'Bryan et al. 2000; Riddell and Tett 2001; ALI 2004; Beyer et al. 2004).

2.4 Health and social care policy

Much recent legislation in this area has been cross-departmental and directed towards the government's aim of creating 'joined up thinking' across government and local departments. For example, the 1989 Children's Act (DoH 1989) and the 2001 Children (Leaving Care) Act (DoH 2001a) have been superseded by the 2004 Children Act (DfES 2004c, see below).

Two important Health and Social Care policy initiatives are relevant to transition. The first has been the introduction of direct payments to people with disabilities, including young people aged 16 and over. This enables them to purchase services for themselves such as employing a personal assistant or organizing their own everyday activities rather than relying on the statutory services to do this for them. Young people can have access to advocacy support where necessary which must be separate from that which is offered to their parents.

Second, the Department of Health's white paper, *Valuing People: A New Strategy for Learning Disability for the 21st Century* (DoH 2001b), also singled out the transition period from school for particular consideration, describing the phase as often 'stressful and difficult' for families and young people. It recommended that people with learning disabilities should have more control and choice over the direction of their lives and that in future services should be developed in the light of person-centred planning. Local Learning Disability Partnership Boards have been established with a remit to create more effective links between child and adult services. Each Board must appoint a Transition Champion responsible for ensuring that transition issues remain on the agenda and that plans are developed for improving transition.

Implementing such a radical agenda has of course met with difficulties. Mansell and Beadle-Brown (2004) and Routledge and Gitsham (2004) suggest that the person's voice and/or that of their families is often lost in the bureaucracy of person-centred planning processes and overridden by the taken for granted assumptions of professionals. Instead person-centred planning is already in danger of becoming a bureaucratic hoop that has little to do with the person's own dreams and ambitions and the services and support that they receive. They suggest that rather than measuring quality by the number of plans completed more emphasis should be placed on the inherent quality of the plans and staff skills.

Valuing People (DoH 2001b) also stressed the need for increased participation in education and training leading to employment and fulfilled adult lives but circumvented the implications for post-16 education and training providers. As Maudslay (2003) points out, developing more person-centred approaches challenges the way in which post-school education and training is organized as well as professional assumptions about the kind of programmes on offer. Traditionally post-school education offers courses with predetermined content and with distinct starting and endpoints. If this is to change, in line with the *Valuing People* recommendations, college managers are concerned that colleges may become alternative day centres as these are closed down. Maudslay concludes, 'Time needs to be given to exploring such different ways of working' (2003: 10).

2.5 Interdepartmental policy

Every Child Matters (DfES 2003a)

The future of Children's Services was outlined in the green paper, *Every Child Matters*. This paper identified five central outcomes for children that lie at the heart of the policy agenda. These are for children to:

- Be healthy
- Stay safe
- Enjoy and achieve

- Make a positive contribution
- Achieve economic well-being

A number of key initiatives sprang from this report designed to strengthen the passage and transfer of information between services and to improve planning for individuals: Children's Trusts, the National Service Framework (DoH 2004), the Children Act 2004 (DfES 2004c) and *Youth Matters* (DfES 2004d). Every English local authority and health service must create a framework, called Children's Trusts, to unify or coordinate their services to children. The National Service Framework sets out quality standards against which these services will be inspected. Standard 4 states, 'All young people have access to age-appropriate services which are responsive to their specific needs as they grow into adulthood'. The statements underpinning this standard emphasize the coordination of services, the centrality of the young person, holistic responses and careful planning.

The Children Act 2004 seeks to improve collaborative working across education, health and social services. For the purposes of the Act children are defined as including young people with learning disabilities up to the age of 20 which may extend to age 25 in certain circumstances. Among the Act's recommendations each authority must produce a unified Children and Young People's Plan, that sets out how the authority intends to discharge its responsibilities in meeting the five outcomes listed in *Every Child Matters*. The Act also requires an integrated inspection framework to be established between education and social services. Registers of disabled children and young people are required to be kept and the Children Act in particular stresses the importance of listening to the young person's perspective throughout the planning process.

The impact of this new legislation remains to be seen but it has the potential to improve and strengthen the links and pathways between child and adult services and school and post-school education and training. Planning together may encourage services to pool resources which in turn may circumvent arguments about who will fund post-school provision. There are two important issues. First, will the need for a single strategic plan lead to the development of a single individual plan for each young person rather than the plethora of plans that now exist? Currently these include plans for transition, care, health, learning, person-centred plans and Connexions Service action plans. Second, the future of the Connexions Service is unclear. Guidance suggests that the new Children's Trusts should take over the management of Connexions partnerships where they are judged to have been successful but how this will work and the impact of this arrangement on a relatively new service that has already experienced a number of upheavals remains to be seen. And who will discharge the responsibilities of the Connexions Services where they are not retained?

Youth Matters (DfES 2004d)

The final response to *Every Child Matters* is the Green Paper *Youth Matters*. This describes the future of services for young people. It attempts to link the work of a number of services together including the Youth Service, Connexions, mainstream leisure and recreational services and targeted support programmes. The proposals are aiming to open up and expand leisure and sporting facilities as well as opportunities for volunteering and other community-based projects. The paper also outlines the future of the Connexions Service. Since its inception there has been an ambivalence about how universal Connexions can be given its limited resources and its mandate to work with targeted groups of young people deemed to be at risk of social exclusion. But many schools have complained about the loss of a universal careers service that works with everyone. Connexions is to be reorganized and its funds given to local authorities from 2008. The third major strand of the proposals relates to support for individual young people who have major social problems and who are not in education, employment or training.

Disability Discrimination Act (DDA) 1996 and the Special Educational Needs and Disability Discrimination Act 2001 (HMSO, 1996; 2001)

Two recent Acts have the potential to widen education, training, employment and social opportunities for young people with special educational needs. Part 4 of the Special Educational Needs and Disability Discrimination Act 2001 extended the 1996 Disability Discrimination Act (DDA) to include education. Education and training providers now have a duty to make reasonable adjustments to ensure that people with disabilities are not discriminated against or treated less favourably than non-disabled students. Colleges and universities have a duty to anticipate applications from and admissions of people with disabilities and should prepare accordingly. If disabled people feel that they are being discriminated against then they have the right to take their case to court, once they have explored all other avenues.

The Disability Equality Scheme extends the duty to ensure equality of opportunity for disabled people to the whole of the public sector. Each public body is expected to produce a scheme that will set out how it intends to comply with this duty.

2.6 Conclusions

Despite laudable intentions the gap between policy and practice remains wide. Policies are, according to Ball, 'representations which are encoded in

complex ways (via struggles, compromises, authoritative public interpretations and reinterpretations) and decoded in complex ways (via actors' interpretations and reinterpretations in relation to their history, experiences,
skills, resources and context)' (1994: 16). In other words, the experiences of
those whom policies are meant to benefit may well differ considerably from
policy intentions. And although time has passed since the events described in
this book took place the reality for many young people and their families
remains the same. This book aims to explore the gap between policy and
practice through the experiences of 12 young people, their families and those
who support them and in the next chapter I explore the kind of decisions that
were made, how they were made and who was involved.

Improving transition planning

1   How much do you know about the work of other services with respect to
    transition?
2   What are the implications of these new policies for the ways in which you
    currently work?
3   What new opportunities might they open up for the young people with
    whom you work?

3 How the decisions were made

3.1 Introduction

In this chapter I explore the kinds of decisions that the young people and their families were making and how they were made. Broadly speaking, ideas about how decisions are made fall into two schools of thought: *normative* and *descriptive* (Bell et al. 1988). Baron (1988) describes *normative* theory as 'the theory of how we should choose among possible actions under ideal conditions. The best decision . . . is the one that best helps us to achieve our goals' (p. 48). Individuals weigh up the pros and cons of various courses of action using the information available to them. Governmental careers guidance and transition planning policies have been strongly influenced by normative or rational theories.

Descriptive approaches describe how people make decisions rather than how they should behave (Mellers et al. 1998). Descriptive models emphasize the messiness of the process and the potential for stress and anxiety. Decision making is influenced as much by affective and personality factors and past experiences as by logic. The extent to which we are motivated to make a decision is influenced by whether we feel in control and whether we feel that we are being presented with a genuine choice.

Why is it necessary to explore ideas about decision making in general in order to understand decision making during the transition from school? Jenkinson (1993) suggests that understanding more about the nature of general decision making helps professionals to provide better support both through how options are presented and by reducing the negative impact of external factors such as legal requirements or economic constraints. The bureaucracy associated with the decision-making processes can dominate and mask the complexity of what young people and their parents or carers are experiencing. The temptation to 'get the forms filled in' can distort proceedings to such an extent that the normal feelings of anxiety and worry that everyone experiences when making major life decisions are ignored and individual voices get lost. And yet what those voices have to say have the potential to make a profound difference to the decisions that are taken, the plans that are made and the nature of the support that is offered.

3.2 What kind of decisions?

The Appendix provides a summary of the profiles of the young people whose stories are told in this book and who were introduced in the first chapter. Since all the students were preparing to leave school, the decisions that they and/or their parents or carers faced were directly or indirectly related to their current or post-school lives. Arguably, decision-making implies making a choice between a range of options. In reality genuine choices for many people with learning difficulties and/or disabilities are limited by attitudinal, practical and logistical barriers. Many of the choices the young people in this study faced are better described as dilemmas where the choice was between remaining within the system and following the route dictated by custom and practice, largely determined by the type of placement they were attending, or the unknown and uncertain alternatives which lay beyond.

For half the students and their parents the decisions concerned residential placements. For Andrew, David, James, Sandra, Nasreen, Maria and their families this meant deciding between local or residential provision and then between colleges. At the same time, Andrew, David, Nasreen and James were also thinking about their longer term job prospects and the best course to take – should Nasreen become a psychologist or a barrister and if so what were the implications for her choice of A levels? What were Andrew's employment prospects if he chose to do an electronics course and would David ever get a job as an actor if he did a drama course? If James could not become a policeman then what could he do? These were the choices and uncertain outcomes they faced.

For Stuart, Costas, Malcolm and their families the choice was whether they should remain in education or try to get a job. Differences between the assumptions of their respective schools became apparent. The Special Educational Needs Co-ordinator (SENCO) at Stuart's comprehensive school assumed that he would leave at 16 and go to college. Yet staff at Costas' and Malcolm's special schools believed that they would each remain in the school's upper secondary department for as long as possible before proceeding to college. For Kim's parents and teachers the main decision was whether she should begin to travel independently. Kim's priority concerned her social life and whether to join the local youth club.

Outwardly, Kylie and Gavin were deciding on Key Stage 4 options and what they wanted to do when they left school. In practice these decisions were gradually subsumed by other more pressing events in their lives that led to them both dropping out of school.

3.3 How the decisions were made

Despite the predictability of many of these decisions, their true complexity is only revealed by looking more closely at the process itself. This book is not so concerned with the kind of choices that are made, and the student's destinations, but *how* decisions are made. In common with other research in this area the picture that emerges is of a process characterized in most cases by fragmentation, uncertainty and confusion (Heslop et al. 2002; Dewson et al. 2004).

Table 3.1 describes the nature of these processes suggesting seven possible patterns of decision making. The processes are grouped along a continuum of intention ranging from those which were conscious decisions where the participants were fully engaged with what was being decided to those where what happened in the end was by default. The right hand column shows the names of the students whose stories best typify each of the different processes.

Table 3.1 Range of decision-making types

	Type	Name
1	Consensus decisions in which options are explored and negotiated over time	Andrew
2	Decisions that appear to be negotiated although some opinions are not acknowledged	Costas David
3	Decisions that are made but then are modified by unexpected, external events	Nasreen
4	Incremental decisions in which one decision depends on the outcomes of another	James
5	Decisions that are made by individuals with or without the agreement of others and which are acted upon alone	Maria Sandra Stuart
6	Decisions made by individuals that are blocked by others	Kim
7	Decisions made by default	Kylie Gavin Malcolm

These different patterns of decision-making processes are not of course mutually exclusive. Several types were sometimes combined to reach a particular outcome. For example, a decision may not be acted on because of differences of opinion between the main players (Type 6) but then an unexpected event can overcome the stumbling block and action is taken whether or not everyone agrees (Type 5). Or a decision may appear to have been taken (Type 2) but then an unexpected event provides an individual with the excuse they have been looking for to assert their viewpoint (Type 5). The vignettes which follow illustrate these different decision-making processes and describe events as they unfolded over the course of the three years.

Consensus decision making (Type 1)

These are decisions where agreement is built up over time during which options are systematically explored and where the key players are actively engaged in the process. The task is then to ensure that decisions are enacted. Andrew Bailey's story was the only one which followed this ideal path.

There seemed to be an unspoken agreement from the beginning between Andrew's parents and his teacher that the most appropriate destination for Andrew on leaving school would be a residential college for deaf and hearing impaired students. For them, the only question was which one? Andrew already had some idea about the subjects he needed to study to become an electrician and he knew he needed to go to college to obtain a qualification, but he was clearly surprised to learn about the existence of local colleges during our interview.

> *Int:*   Do you want to go away to college or go to one near your home?
> *Andrew:*   [writing] I don't know. I want to know what it look like.
> *Int:*   Do you mean you want to know what the college looks like?
> *Andrew:*   [writing] I like it or don't like it ... Do you know where college is near my home?

But his mother had discussed the local college with a friend:

> I began to learn different stories about it and I think it is a normal college but there is a group of people she [her friend] works with ... a few of them are deaf and the rest aren't but they are all what we call mature students, I think, not 16 to 18 ones. I think they tend to be 20 up to 30 and they are all mentally retarded and some of them just happen to be deaf as well and I thought if that is the only facility ... I don't agree with them all being in a class together.

His parents wanted Andrew to be with those they considered his intellectual equals and with whom he could communicate. They preferred the residential specialist college recommended by Andrew's teacher, where he would live with hearing impaired students but study at a local college.

Andrew however was not convinced and during his Year 10 review, he said he was undecided whether to go to a local or residential college. Andrew insisted on visiting two local colleges before making up his mind but in the end, Andrew chose the residential option. However, as both local colleges had offered him a place the funding agency were less likely to fund the specialist college option. Andrew and his family were held in suspense until just before he left school when they heard that their application for funding had been successful.

So, a decision was reached over time that met the approval of all. Obstacles were overcome and a feeling of solidarity built up as they man-euvered their way through the bureaucratic procedures. Nevertheless Andrew only received information about local colleges as a result of his meeting with me. By withholding information either consciously or unconsciously his parents and teachers had not regarded him as an equal partner in the deci-sion-making process.

Quasi-negotiated decisions – 'Going round in circles' (Type 2)

In some cases decisions were reached despite there being no real exploration of the different opinions held by the various participants. For example David's father was adamant from the earliest discussions that David must go to a residential college and he was not prepared to listen to any alternative perspectives. For Costas and his parents the decision to remain at school appeared to be negotiated but on closer examination differing views were not fully explored even though a decision was eventually taken.

His teachers and careers adviser felt Costas should remain at school when he reached 16. His parents, however, were dissatisfied with the school feeling that he was held back by other pupils and that expectations were too low. His father wanted him to learn a trade, although his mother judged this to be beyond Costas' capabilities. In his Year 11 annual review his mother raised the possibility of him leaving school. She had been told by a neighbour about a full-time employment training scheme run by Marks and Spencer but the deputy head was not convinced.

> *Deputy head:*   Personally I wouldn't recommend he leaves now. He needs to get more confidence – he'll have a say about where he wants to go. We will work with the Careers service . . . she'll get to know him. She'll come to a meeting like this.
>
> *Mother:*   Listen, I don't know . . . I only suggested.
>
> *Teacher:*   Still it's an interesting opportunity – he could go to M and S.

Having made the suggestion, Mrs Demetrios was covered with confusion and backed down, rapidly agreeing that Costas should stay at school and do a work experience placement instead. Nevertheless, she wanted to know more about the scheme.

Costas, for his part, was unclear what he wanted to do. By his Year 12 review the decision as to whether Costas should leave school was back on the agenda. Mrs Demetrios was still keen on the Marks and Spencer's option, where Costas had worked for a day. If he was to leave the school staff thought college was a better option but Costas was confused, saying at one point, 'My head's going round in circles'. Despite his parents' wishes it was agreed that Costas would remain at school for a further year. Mrs Demetrios hoped he would eventually get a place on the Marks and Spencer's scheme; his father still wanted him to 'get a trade'. Costas remained uncertain.

At one level it could be argued that Costas had no real choices. There was no guarantee that he would get a place on a work training scheme or that this would lead to a job, yet his parents were driven by their dissatisfaction and disappointment in the education system. The concerns of his parents were never fully explored, despite the fact that Costas's Year 10 teacher shared many of their reservations about his placement at the school. Costas felt torn between his home and school not really knowing what to think. In the end Costas remained in education eventually leaving school to go to college.

'Fate takes a hand' (Type 3)

There were several examples of chance or unexpected events pushing decisions in one direction or another. Sometimes, as in the cases of Maria, Sandra and Stuart, sudden events confirmed an individual's preferred course of action. In other instances such events helped to transform or modify decisions that had already been negotiated. The decision of Nasreen to stay at college for three years is an example of how initially well-defined plans can become modified by subsequent events but also how disturbing events can be used to advantage.

Nasreen's ambition was to become a clinical psychologist. To achieve this, she planned to go to university after attending a residential specialist college to do four A level examinations: biology, sociology, English literature and history. She described her interest in psychology as stemming from her own experiences of counselling. She believed she could provide a source of solace and comfort to others and gave the reasons for her wish to study psychology as follows:

> As a child I suffered horrible depression, I don't know the reason for it and for that reason I would not like others to go through what I have been through. I have often contemplated suicide for example. It has been quite bad ... because I think integration was also the cause because they said by the way you are going to be integrated next year, get used to the fact ... and I think it is partly because I want to study psychology to understand what goes on in the scenes behind the mind ... Often it gives me a lot of pleasure to listen to other

people and try to get their problems out into the open, simply because I know exactly what they are suffering.

Having obtained the required grades in her GCSEs, Nasreen went on to a residential college as planned and followed three of her four chosen A level courses. However, in her second year she was told that she must have one of her eyes removed. This was devastating news. An earlier operation had gone wrong and this was apparently the only option. Noting how carefully she had mapped out her course of action she commented, 'Isn't it amazing how things change so quickly?'

Nasreen decided to stay on at college a third year, to spread out her three A levels and to take an additional A/S level. She had taken part in some mock trials which had rekindled an earlier interest in the law and she was now considering becoming a barrister. So she thought she might take a psychology degree at university followed by a six-month conversion course to law. As she said, 'Sometimes fate takes a hand and you get pulled down to earth. But I am trying to see something positive in a negative situation'. She used the operation as an opportunity to strengthen her chances of getting into university, particularly as she wanted to widen her career options.

This chain of events caused Nasreen to alter her planned course of action but she used the changes to gain some possible longer term advantages. Instead of closing down opportunities, she was using her enforced extra year at college to widen her career options.

Incremental decisions or a 'leap in the dark' (Type 4)

These are decisions where one decision is predicated on another, i.e., unless we decide what to do about A we cannot decide what to do about B. In James Simpson's case because he could not decide what he wanted to do as a job he did not know what course to take. Lack of information, which led to difficulties in seeing a way forward, characterized the decisions surrounding James and his future. James' father, in describing his feelings about the process, noted, 'That's the difficulty – actually seeing the direction'. When James was 12 or 13 his mother had begun worrying about what James would do when he left school. She noted,

> I asked to see someone in careers a couple of years ago, because I was that worried about what he could do and she more or less said come back when he is a little older. I can't do anything yet. It seems to be the on-going thing you know, we will look at it soon but not just yet.

Mr and Mrs Simpson had very little information about James' longer term options, and what he would do in the sixth form.

> I would like some idea about what James will be doing in the sixth form and where he is going to after the sixth form because we are coming up to a big jump now from the fifth year to the sixth form. I have been told there is a change in the way things work but I don't really know what it is, so I would like to have more information on that and as I say what the options are college wise.

Above all his parents were anxious that James became as independent as possible, with a

> proper job, not sort of sitting in a sheltered workshop type place, I would like him to be out in the real world working with normal people and doing something that will make him happy. That is what I really want, I want him to be happy at the end of the day.

Consequently his mother was very disappointed when, at his Year 11 review, any attempts to discuss James's longer term options were curtailed. His teacher said that she envisaged that James would go to a residential college but that in the first instance James would join the sixth form. His mother requested more information about the sixth form and the possibility of James getting a Saturday job. However, the teacher replied that they would receive the information 'in time'.

In the following year the annual review meeting proceeded with an undercurrent of irritation as James' father asked three times for an explanation of what he referred to as 'gobbledy gook' in various reports. His father was confused about the direction James should be taking. According to his teacher James had chosen to follow a business studies course at the local secondary school. His work experience in a local office was to be delayed because James was due to have a major operation. Meanwhile the school was still without a careers adviser. Talking to his parents later in the year, they both wanted James to pursue a vocational qualification but felt helpless about what to advise him.

In his statement for his Year 13 annual review James wrote, 'I am hoping to go to a College away from home so that I can do more things for myself and so that I can do a BTEC Business Studies Course'. But during the meeting Mrs Evans, James' teacher, revealed that she thought James' poor paper management and organization skills would prevent him from taking such a course. It was now only five months before James was due to leave school and his father, clearly irritated, questioned why James had been directed to follow a business studies programme when his organizational skills were apparently so poor.

By the time James came to leave school, the issue of which course to follow had still not been resolved.

Father: We've never really resolved the issue as to whether, because he wasn't so good at organizational skills, he would be better to avoid them completely or to work on them . . . That's one of the things I wanted to try and sort out with the teacher, but we never really got to that situation whether it was worth working on or whether to abandon the whole thing.

Mother: I think we went up to Barnwood College [a residential college] after that anyway and when they did their assessment they came up with IT.

Father: I think its part of the business studies course anyway, and it honed down to be the best subject for him to study out of the business studies course and then he could always broaden out later.

So in the end James and his parents took a leap in the dark and followed the advice of his new college. They were still uncertain about what James' longer term future would hold but in the end this decision and what course he should take took second place to securing a residential college placement.

The lone decision maker – 'Alone in the world' (Type 5)

In contrast to collective decision making, some decisions were made in isolation. Stuart decided that the careers service and the local college had been so slow in organizing a placement for him that he found himself a job. Similarly Sandra's parents were so determined that Sandra should attend local provision, despite the opinions of everyone else, that when they discovered a local programme they arranged for her enrolment. Maria's mother, Mrs Constandis, operated almost entirely alone in choosing Maria's post-school provision.

It became clear from my first meeting with her when Maria was in Year 12 that Mrs Constandis was considering residential provision. She thought that the quality of local provision was poor:

> I don't trust what they say, put it this way, here, within the borough, they have so many changes. All the time it is different, you go through accountants, social workers, policies have changed, there is no funds or they are suddenly cut off and your morale just zooms down.

The Rhetts Syndrome Association was opening a new four-place home outside London and, despite the distance, she wanted Maria to go there. For her, the decision was becoming not whether to apply but when: 'The problem is how long do I wait, how much do I wait because you don't often get vacancies so it is a very big problem for me to decide what to do'.

Three months later, at Maria's annual review, the issue of where Maria would go on leaving school was raised. The discussion was dominated by the social worker who warned of difficulties in funding residential placements and instead described various combinations of local day centre and care home provision. He had arranged for day care staff to visit the school to meet Maria. No further discussion of the residential option took place. Later when I asked Mrs Constandis about this she replied that as the placement she had in mind was not 'educational' she did not think it appropriate to discuss her ideas in the meeting.

Later that year when Mrs Constandis returned from her summer holiday to collect Maria from the local care home she was shocked to find her thin and malnourished. Mrs Constandis attributed this to care staff failing to feed Maria properly. Then, in the following January, Maria was badly scalded while having a shower and for Mrs Constandis this was the final straw. Straightaway she filled in the application form for the residential home and sent it off.

Maria was offered a place immediately and left school a month later. Unaware that a residential home was being considered her teacher said she was 'cheated, rushed and shocked'. She described Mrs Constandis as feeling 'as if she's all alone in the world with Maria'. The school felt helpless and unable to comfort Maria whose distress increased as the time approached for her to leave school. Her teacher believed that Maria did not want to leave home but went on, 'How far do you go in giving them real choices over major decisions … if you know that it isn't possible to give real choice?'

The decision for Maria to go to a residential placement was almost entirely that of Maria's mother. In her desire to do the best for her daughter she acted alone, failing to recognize Maria's need to be involved in the process. While Maria may not have had many choices there were steps that the school could have taken to prepare Maria for leaving had they been aware of what was happening. But Maria's mother believed herself to be solely responsible for Maria's future and did not trust the services to support her or her daughter. From Mrs Constandis' perspective there was simply no point in involving anyone else in the process.

Decisions that are made but not enacted (Type 6)

Some decisions were made by individuals but for a variety of reasons were not realized. Kim Doyle wanted to join a youth club but her parents would not allow it. While this decision is of a different order from those discussed so far, it was significant for Kim.

Kim was 16 when I first met her and her wish to join a youth club emerged during my second meeting with her at school. It resurfaced when I met her parents later the same year. Her mother objected to the idea saying that Kim would get overtired and that she might be abused or attacked in the street. Mr Doyle, recognizing Kim's growing adolescence, acknowledged their problem in accepting that Kim was now a teenager.

Three months later at Kim's annual review, the following exchange took place as the meeting wound to a close:

Deputy head:	Mr and Mrs Doyle, is there anything else?
Kim:	Club. Don't go to club on Thursday.
Father:	Not really, we're only getting involved with our fears.
Mother:	Not really.
Kim:	Club – don't go to club on Thursday only go in the summer.
Mother:	Groom Street Club runs on Thursdays. That's when I can help all my children. She keeps asking me. I said no to going to a club.
Deputy head:	It's good that Mum can spend time with you.

Here Kim attempts to use the review meeting to air her views. Even though she repeats herself, her request was not given any serious consideration. Instead, the deputy headteacher went along with Mrs Doyle's objections, giving no time to exploring Kim's aspiration. Then she suggested that Mrs Doyle should take responsibility for helping Kim to join a youth club, something that her mother would be extremely reluctant to do given her anxieties about Kim's safety.

At the next review, the issue of the youth club was not mentioned despite the fact that it was part of the action plan. When questioned afterwards Mrs Doyle said that now the timings of the club interfered with their mealtimes. Why was Kim's wish never realized? Were the teachers afraid of tackling Mrs Doyle's deep-rooted fears? Did the fact that it was Kim's action point give it lower status? Was it so unusual for a student to make a request that it was outside the teachers' frame of reference or was it really just an oversight? The answer probably lies in all four explanations.

So in the end, despite her attempts to assert herself, Kim did not go to the youth club. To ensure that something happens as the result of a personal decision it is either necessary to have some status and power within the decision-making group or to have the personal capacity to take action oneself. Kim possessed neither of these and no one was prepared to act as an advocate on her behalf.

Decisions made by default – a sense of destiny (Type 7)

Some decisions were not conscious decisions at all but instead were drifted into on the tide of events. Each example of this form of decision making involved young people dropping out of school: Gavin, Malcolm and Kylie.

That Kylie would drop out of her comprehensive school was an overriding concern for the SENCO from the first time we met when Kylie was in Year 9. I met her mother when Kylie was 15 and she was also concerned that her daughter would repeat what she saw as the mistakes she had made as a teenager by dropping out of school and getting married at 17. So there was a sense of foreboding on the part of her mother and her teacher about Kylie's destiny.

Kylie was insightful about her future career aspirations. Early conversations revealed her desire to work with computers (although she thought her basic skills were not good enough), work with animals (although someone had told her the training was very long) or work with children. At our third meeting, by which time she had dropped out of school and was doing work experience at a nursery school, she thought that she needed to improve her English and mathematics to train as a nursery nurse.

By the time she was 13, Kylie's pattern of attendance had already become patchy. She had gone through a period of being a school refuser described by the SENCO as follows,

> She has been going through a stage, it has stopped at the moment, whereby she has tendencies to becoming a school refuser. She was always being ill, and away a great deal and that is simply because she can't access the lessons. She simply got fed up of it . . . If everything is too hard and too fast for you, you eventually wear out . . . Lots of family illness, so Kylie's attendance was interrupted. She gets depressed about not being able to work in school, and she gets stomach aches and headaches. She is a worrier. Little problems become big problems.

The SENCO felt that Kylie should have gone to a school for children with moderate learning difficulties. She had advised her colleagues on ways of modifying their teaching but many were unwilling to accommodate Kylie's needs and instead Kylie was withdrawn from class for the majority of time.

So why did she begin to drop out again? The SENCO believed that Kylie was afraid of failing her GCSE examinations, but was this the only reason? Kylie herself said that she found it difficult to go back to school if she missed a day, that school was noisy and she knew others who did not attend school. On the other hand, she missed her friends. The situation with her three brothers had also deteriorated – the oldest had periods of absenteeism and suspension from school, her 9-year-old brother had been expelled from school, he was extorting money from his mother and he had been caught stealing and begging from neighbours. His 5-year-old brother was now copying him. Mrs Long, who had split up from her boyfriend, was working at the local pub while Kylie was left to take care of her brothers.

The school had arranged a work placement for Kylie at a nursery for two days a week, combined with some home tutoring, which at her Year 11 annual review (held at her home) was reported as going well. There was a sense throughout the meeting, however, that her teacher and the careers adviser were struggling to keep Kylie in the system which she was resisting. By March of the same year Kylie had been invited to extend her time at the nursery to almost full-time and everyone, including Joyce Gray, was delighted, but by June the arrangement had collapsed. A familiar pattern of behaviour had emerged as Kylie began well, started to arrive late and then went through extended periods of absenteeism. Her teacher speculated that her inability to get up in the morning was related to depression caused by the spiralling difficulties at home. When the boys were younger Kylie could cope with their behaviour, but as they became older and more out of control she withdrew into herself. The burden of responsibility as the eldest and only daughter had become too great for her to bear and in the end she left school through default rather than through making an active choice.

3.4 Conclusions

The examples described here have been arranged along a continuum of intentionality and conscious decision making. They each describe the degrees of involvement and personal agency of the different players in what Ball et al. (2000: 144) describe as the 'choreography of decision-making'. Many of the experiences during the decision-making process were similar to those of the young people described in Hodkinson et al.'s (1996) and Ball et al.'s (2000) research. There were the same tensions and complex interplay between personal determination and the pressure of external assumptions and structures in pre-determining what they would do when they left school. It would be wrong to assume however that the process is identical. In my final interview with her Nasreen had asked, 'Am I the same [as others]?' but as Morris states, 'Transition to adulthood for young disabled people is both the same and different as it is for nondisabled young people' (1999: 24). Professionals need to recognize and respond to both the similarities and the differences.

A distinguishing feature of the decision-making process for young people with special educational needs is the formality of the procedures with which they, their families and the professionals are expected to engage. Whereas decision making is largely, though not entirely, a private process for everyone else, pupils with special educational needs are subject to more regular official scrutiny and debate than other young people. Decision making for them has become a public process. The extent to which these formal procedures actually support the process is debatable (Tisdall 1996; Wood and Trickey 1996; Miner and Bates 1997; Heslop et al. 2002; Dewson et al. 2004). During these procedures the students and their families were often subjected to external pressures and professional assumptions about their options, which sometimes led to confusion and misunderstandings. Meetings tended to focus on the completion of formalities rather than spending time genuinely exploring anxieties or possibilities. When asked to comment on the usefulness of the meetings, 5 out of 11 parents expressed disappointment as compared to 3 out of 24 professionals.

In line with other research, status and power emerged as significant issues in the meetings (Riddell et al. 1994; Armstrong 1995; Reay 1996; Wilkinson 2000; Smart 2004). Examples include the power of a parent over a child, father over mother or the school over parents and it was clear that some individuals were accorded higher status than others. Parents' views were more likely to be listened to than those of pupils. Some types of decisions were also accorded greater priority – Kim's wish to attend the youth club was not seen as being as important as the decision over whether she should travel independently. Yet the two things were inextricably linked. Was this to do with Kim's place in the pecking order or was it to do with the nature of her concern? Probably both. James' aspiration to get a Saturday job was never discussed and neither was Mrs Demetrios' suggestion about exploring Marks and Spencer's training programmes given any serious consideration.

The relative power of individuals within the process was determined by their access to information, a point made by Wilkinson (2000). Parents of children with disabilities are at a great disadvantage in relation to professionals since, as well as often feeling sensitive to the risks involved in asking questions or challenging opinions, parents are dependent on professionals for access to information and resources. Information was withheld by parents and teachers from children (Andrew), by teachers from parents (Mr and Mrs Simpson) and by parents from teachers (Mrs Constandis). Like the parents in Wilkinson's study, Mrs Constandis derived her information, and consequently her power, from belonging to a voluntary organization, as well as through her membership of various local committees. More often parents relied on friends, family and other parents for advice and information, a point to which I return in Chapter 5.

Finally this analysis of patterns of decision making raises questions about the place of formal review meetings in resolving difficult and complex issues. On several occasions the underlying issues and concerns were brushed aside because of the formality of the setting, as for example in Kim's case. Some parents opted out (Mrs Constandis, Mrs Demetrios) while others became angry (Mr Simpson, Mr Francis). The meetings themselves are crude instruments for exploring many of the issues that crop up. Both careful planning beforehand involving the young person and their parents or carers as well as sustained support afterwards is required. Some commentators have gone so far as to suggest that these formal meetings have outlived their usefulness and that more radical approaches are required that genuinely place young people in the driving seat. These are discussed in Chapter 6.

Underlying each of these stories was a complex interaction of factors and as Hodkinson and Sparkes (1997) put it, 'The decision-making was context related, and could not be separated from the family background, culture and life histories of the pupils' (p. 33). A closer examination of these contextual influences forms the focus of the next three chapters, beginning with the young people's perspectives.

Note

An earlier version of this chapter appeared in the *Journal of Research in Special Educational Needs*, June 2002, 2(2).

Improving transition planning

1   Working in groups of three or four individually read through one of the case studies. Then discuss the following questions:
   • Who was involved?
   • Who or what had the most influence on what happened?
   • What struck you about the process?
   • If you had been one of the professionals involved how might you have responded?
   • Would you have done anything differently?
2   Working on your own, identify a student who left school or college last year and then make a note of
   • what they went on to do;
   • what you understood their aspirations to be;
   • what their parents or carers wanted to happen;
   • what you wanted to happen;
   • any significant events that occurred – these could be positive or negative and could be related, for example, to the student's interests, achievements, health or family. Now identify which of these factors helped or hindered the decision-making processes.
   Now compare your analysis with a partner and identify any common factors or issues that emerge. Be prepared to feed these back to other members of your group. What could have been done to strengthen the influence of positive factors and reduce the impact of negative factors?
3   If you work with young people with profound and complex learning diffi-culties ensure that you build in opportunities that enable them to get used to change and choice in their lives. Many ideas can be found in *Enhancing Quality of Life: Facilitating Transitions for People with Profound and Complex Learning Difficulties* (Byers et al. 2002). Here are a few suggestions:

- Celebrate when people leave through award ceremonies, farewell parties, giving cards and gifts.
- Use communication passports to pass on information to others about the learner's likes and dislikes, learning preferences, strategies for behaviour management.
- Encourage new and unfamiliar staff to spend time learning how individuals prefer to communicate.
- Ensure that learners are supported by people who know them well and who can make suggestions about their preferences, dreams and aspirations.

4   The young people's stories

4.1 Introduction

The next three chapters explore the process of decision making in more detail from three perspectives: the young person's, their parents or carers and the professionals who support them. Before looking at each of these in more detail, I want to set the discussion in the ideas of Bronfenbrenner's ecosystemic theory. Norwich (2000) locates Bronfenbrenner's ecosystemic theory in the broad school of organismic psychology (as opposed to mechanistic or individualistic approaches) in which the individual cannot be separated from their context, so that the whole is greater than and different from the sum of the individual parts. Bronfenbrenner (1979) and Bronfenbrenner and Morris (1998), envisage society as a series of 'nested systems' rather like a Russian doll, beginning at the micro level of, for example, the person in the family and moving through to school or college and community to the macro levels of the wider society and culture. Individuals can be members of different microsystems such as their youth group, their residential home or their teaching group. Each system has its own dynamic, which in turn relates to and is influenced by the others. These relationships are described as mesosystems. The usefulness of Bronfenbrenner's framework for looking at what happens during the decision-making process lies partly in his focus on the roles that individuals adopt and the relationships between individuals, systems and organizations. In this study I have referred to the decision-making unit as consisting of the young person, their family, and teachers and other professionals. However, using ecosystemic theory, this unit could be said to constitute a mesosystem since in Bronfenbrenner's terms the so-called unit spanned two microsystems: the family and the school.

Building on an earlier model developed by Christenson and Sheridan (2001) their different, and sometimes conflicting, perspectives are summarized in Figure 4.1. The relationships between the parents and their child within the family microsystem were dominated by the parents' perception of their role as carer and their anxieties about the future and their desires for their children to be safe and happy. This in turn limited the freedoms that some parents felt able to ascribe to their children, for example to go out with friends, to travel independently, to go to a youth club, to prepare for change. Most parents struggled with the need to give their child more autonomy

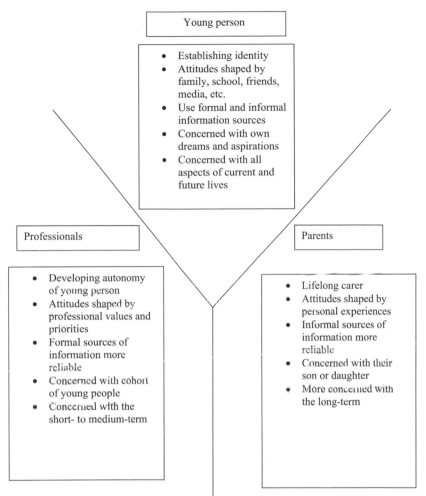

Figure 4.1 Perspectives on transition

while retaining their belief in their child's dependence and it was this struggle that dominated the nature of many of the relationships.

The relationship between parents and professionals was governed by their different perceptions of the transition process, that is as the world existed for each of them within their different roles and their place within the ecosystem. Their individual perspectives were shaped by their past experiences, their roles and responsibilities, how they each construed the young person. While parents saw their role as carers, teachers and other professionals were anxious to develop the young person's autonomy. Professionals also acted as sources of information. This role gave professionals a good deal of power and the extent to which they shared information or recognized parents' need for information was an important influence on relationships during the decision-making process.

The professional–pupil relationship was governed by the professionals perception of the young person and their needs. These perceptions differed between individuals as well as between members of different disciplines, depending on their particular culture and training. But professionals' perception of the transition process is also influenced by factors in the broader macrosystem such as the need to interpret and follow national policies and guidance on transition planning, their knowledge of local education, training and work opportunities, and health and social services support. Their interpretation of these wider national policies are mediated through their own needs and personal agendas.

The young person straddles a number of microsystems particularly home and school or college – they inhabit both worlds. For some, such as Malcolm and Costas, this led to confusion; in others, such as Nasreen, determination; in Kylie and Gavin, resignation or rebellion. Their need to assert their identities as young people was clearly demonstrated in a variety of ways, but the extent to which they were able to do so varied between individuals and between settings. The young people were engaged in what Bronfenbrenner refers to as an 'ecological transition' as they prepared to leave school and move on to the next phase of their lives.

I begin by exploring the decision-making process from the young person's perspective. This chapter explores in more detail the influence *of* as well as the influences *on* the young people as they experienced the decision-making process during their final years of schooling. To begin this chapter, I discuss the processes in which these young people were engaged, i.e., the process of moving from childhood to adulthood.

4.2 Exploring who they are and who they want to become

In thinking and talking about themselves and their future lives, the young people were engaged in a number of different processes summarized here as *expressing, seeking* and *asserting their identities*. In other words they were, as Brannen (1996) describes, engaged not so much 'in being but in becoming' (p. 114). The question then follows, how far did others acknowledge this to be the case? To what extent were they enabled to escape from childhood and be accepted as adolescents?

Of course, to be conscious of self in this way and to be able to express thoughts and ideas demands a high level of self-awareness on the part of individuals as well as sophisticated communication skills. However, by listening carefully to young people's language, through observing them in school and at home and through listening to the accounts of their parents and teachers, I was able to build up a picture of each student. Sometimes they described themselves, their likes and dislikes, that is, they were *expressing their identity*. They also talked about who they wanted to become (*seeking an identity*) and the factors that would either support or inhibit them in this process. These factors helped to shape and structure what have been variously termed their 'zone of possibilities' (Gottfredson 1981), their 'possible and impossible selves' (Oyserman and Markus 1990) or their 'horizons for action' (Hodkinson et al. 1996). Each of these terms suggests a process of exploration, considering, refining or discarding possibilities or, as one of the students in this study described, 'knowing the field'. Finally, like the people with learning difficulties in Riddell et al.'s (1999) research, some young people had decided what they wanted, and made their choices but the extent to which they could influence decisions and assert their preferences often lay in the gift of others. On the scale of things the young people in this study were often relatively powerless and sometimes sought alternative ways to *assert their identity*.

These three dimensions of identity are not separate parts of the process of growing up but merge and interact with each other and are influenced by a complex interplay of other factors. For example, when it came to making up his mind about which college to go to Andrew was clear that both the choice of course and the nature of the other students were important to him. The following interview was conducted through an interpreter:

Int: What did you think about Brayborough College and John Brown College [both sector colleges]?

Andrew: Brayborough had a very small electrical place, the course was small. At John Brown the electrical course was OK but **I would be the only deaf person there and I didn't want that** [my emphasis].

Int: So, in deciding which college to go to, what is the most important thing for you?

Andrew: The course itself.

Int: That is the most important consideration and then next the other students.

Andrew: I wouldn't feel comfortable if I was just **on my own** so **it is important to have both** [my emphasis].

Here Andrew is emphasizing that he wants to be with other deaf students and that he would feel alone without them (expressing identity). However, with an eye on the future, he also wanted to go to a college where he would have the opportunity to mix with hearing people to increase his confidence because his aspiration was to get a job as an electrician in open employment (seeking identity). This is what he wrote: 'If I go to college for deaf only, then get job in future and I will not feel confidence mixed with hearing, if I go to mixed deaf and hearing college I will learn more what they are like. Also I will feel confidence in job in the future.' He was concerned to 'look around and see where the best college for me is'. Later, when he had completed his visits, he dismissed his next annual review as boring because he had made up his mind (asserting identity). Arguably if Andrew had not had a Statement then there would have been no need for further public discussion. He would just have applied to the college of his choice. Ball et al. (2000) aptly summarize this relationship between a young person's identity and the selection of their FE college: 'Choosing a college is in some respects like choosing a way of representing yourself' (2000: 30). Here Andrew is thinking of himself not only as a member of a distinctive deaf community, but also of himself in the future and who he would like to become straddling the deaf and hearing worlds, working in open employment as an electrician in the hearing world. His choice of college was influenced by this desire.

4.3 Influences on choices

Ball et al. (2000) argue that the choices that we make are symptomatic of how we see ourselves. In this section I begin by discussing how the choices that some young people were considering reflected how they saw themselves. But such choices are not made in a vacuum. We are influenced directly or indirectly by a range of other factors in our lives. This group of young people like all others were influenced in their thinking and their preferences by their families; their aspirations, strengths and interests; their gender and ethnicity; their wish to be accorded adolescent or adult status; their friendships or lack of them. Where they differed was the extent to which each of these factors interacted with their disability and/or learning difficulty. This was a constant theme running through most conversations, seeming to impact on and shape much of what happened and the responses to those events. For that reason I have not identified the pupils' special educational needs as a distinctive influence.

Families

There is an assumption that the parents of young people with special educational needs play a much greater role in the decision-making process than those of other youngsters. Again it's a question of degree. Brannen (1996), Hodkinson (1995) and Ball et al. (2000) have all argued that the degree of involvement by families and their influence on young people in the decision-making processes has been underestimated by researchers and that only in the small minority of cases is the family's role insignificant. Other studies

(Morrow and Richards 1996) assert that even where their influence may not be direct, families exert influence through the level of economic and practical support they are able to offer as well as through the continuous socialization processes in which families are engaged.

Parental opinion may supersede any views that their child has, particularly if their child has learning difficulties. So, while the majority of families do participate in the 'choreography of decision-making' (Ball et al. 2000: 144), the opinions of parents of children with learning difficulties are likely to be more dominant, in some cases appearing to exclude or override those of their children's. Now there are many good reasons for this which are explored in more detail in the following chapter. But here we are concerned with the voice of the young person.

Families can also exercise a more indirect and benign influence. There were numerous examples of how families influenced their children and the choices that were made. Family members acted as role models, sources of information and advice or provided links into work opportunities. The family was also the means by which young people were introduced into their cultures and traditions which sometimes, as in Nasreen's case, lead to feelings of fear and confusion about who they were and what their future entailed. The main differences in parental influence appears to be one of degree rather than substance. Even so, like all families, parents and their children varied in their relative degrees of active involvement, as summarized in Figure 4.2.

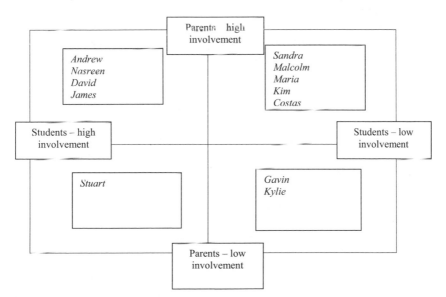

Figure 4.2 Degrees of involvement in the decision-making process (adapted from Brannen 1996)

How can these differences be explained? Brannen's (1996) analysis of the relationship between parents and adolescent children is helpful. Brannen suggests that the ways in which parents construct their children's adolescence influences their relationships with their children, and that in turn influences the degree of autonomy their offspring are afforded. Parents' ideas are governed by a range of other factors including both cultural and gender-related issues, and in this case I would suggest they are also governed by the fact that their child also has a learning difficulty or disability.

In Figure 4.2 the name of the young person indicates their apparent degree of active direct involvement in the decision-making process relative to that of their parents. Whereas there was a high degree of involvement by parents in most cases there was a notable lack of direct involvement by the parents or carers of Stuart, Gavin and Kylie. Conversely there was a high degree of involvement by Nasreen, Andrew, James, David and Stuart but a low direct involvement by the remainder of the casestudy adolescents.

The nature and severity of their child's disability clearly played a powerful and in some instances all-consuming role in constructing parental views about their child's adolescence, the autonomy they ascribed to them now and in their future lives. Disability and other factors that influenced parental responses are explored in greater depth in the next chapter but what concerns us here is the extent to which the role of the family and, more particularly, the parents was so powerful that the young person's identity and consequently their ideas were subsumed. Consequently, in families where there was a high degree of involvement by parents but low autonomy ascribed to the individual young person, it was sometimes almost impossible to distinguish between the views of the parents and those of their child.

Sandra is a case in point. Contrast Sandra's views with those of her mother and teacher. In Sandra's mind leaving school and going to college was synonymous with leaving her home and family, something she did not want to do. At our first meeting, when she was 15, she told me about her fears:

Int: Is there anything that you worry about when you think about leaving school?

Sandra: I'll miss my Mum and Dad.

Int: Will you? Where will you go when you leave school then?

Sandra: To college.

Int: Does that mean you'll have to go away from your Mum and Dad?

Sandra: But I'll still miss them.

Int: Have you been to a college?

Sandra: No.

Int: What do you think it's like? What do you think you do there, do you know?

Sandra: No.

Int: Who told you about it?

Sandra: My mum, my dad and my brother.

Int: They all told you about it, did they? What did they say?

Sandra: They all ... Sandra, we're gonna miss you.

In trying to understand more about Sandra's perspective I turned to her parents and teachers. There were marked differences in how they each perceived her needs and responses. For her mother there was a conflict between treating Sandra as a dependent child for whom she had to provide constant care and protection and as an adolescent, enabling her to assert her own identity. She described her daughter as: 'a smashing little girl'; 'a good little soul'; 'a nervous child'; 'a very innocent little girl' but she recognized that others expected her to afford Sandra more autonomy:

> I hope you don't think we are being selfish. In a way she should be more independent and she's not going to be independent if we don't let her go ... I hope she gets independent. I don't want to stifle her. She's not that child who has got that knowledge so that she can go out on her own. You know you do see people in wheelchairs and they can go out on their own. She could never do that.

Another assumption that professionals sometimes make is to treat parents as if they have one voice. It was true that her parents did not want her to go to a residential college but they disagreed about the alternative. Mrs Harding wanted Sandra to go to specialist local provision, her father wanted her to stay at home preferring the family to take care of everything themselves. This created a dilemma for his wife. She valued her time alone to get on with chores when Sandra stayed overnight at school and in any case she felt her daughter should spend time with her peers. She said:

> I know that when she's there [at school] she's going to be out doing something with the crowd. I think, well, she should be out and if she can stay at college that would be very nice for me whereas Paul wants her here every minute of the day. He doesn't have to do what women have to do and I find that when I come home from work – I know he will have done all the cooking and the shopping and hoovered round – but there's still loads to do.

In contrast, Sandra's teachers believed that she should go to a residential college to decrease her dependency on her parents. One teacher regarded her parents' ideas of residential colleges as 'Dickensian'. It did seem as if a culture of interdependence had developed within the family, arguably driven more by her father's attitudes than her mother's, who in spite of her personal dilemmas, wanted Sandra to build a life outside the home. Six months later Sandra told me that she was 'having a college at home' and that she hoped that she would be able to go off to the pub in the evening with her mother for 'a quiet drink' just as her brother and father did.

Conversely lack of family support can also act as a powerful influence. The need for what he regarded as a real family drove Gavin to re-establish links with his birth father. Once Gavin had found his father he began to treat him as a role model, much to his foster mother's concern as she believed he was a drug dealer. This is how Gavin described relationships with his foster family and his desire to spend more time with his father:

> Gavin: I don't listen to them anymore. They didn't want me to have my ear pierced but I did anyway. I'm allowed to go and see my Dad once a month but I go more often than that. When I'm 18 I'm going to go and live with my Dad.
> Int: What does he do?
> Gavin: Don't know but he's always got lots of money.

He dreamed of having a family – he wanted to get married, have two children and to keep a dog and a snake. He was not allowed to keep pets at his foster home although he loved animals and wanted to work with them. A year later when asked whether he still wished to work with animals, he laughed and was evasive at first:

> Gavin: Well, I would like to work in a zoo but not that much.
> Int: Could you do work experience with animals?
> Gavin: I want to go to the RSPCA but I don't know where to go to find out, I can't be bothered.

Then, pointing to the Yellow Pages,

> Gavin: The number's in there.
> Int: Have you ever talked to anyone about this?
> Gavin: No! Anyway the training's long.
> Int: How do you know?
> Gavin: I was watching a TV programme.

However the school was unaware of these ambitions and there was no one at home to listen to and help him. Gavin lacked what Putnam and Goss (2002) refer to as social capital, important social networks characterized by mutual trust and reciprocity that provide the essential support and security that we all need. There was no one to advocate for Gavin and to provide the kind of indirect influence and support he required to help him achieve his aspirations.

In the end, Gavin had to leave his foster home for stealing and was placed with another family. Then he was excluded from school. He was reported to be living with squatters and I eventually lost touch with him despite efforts to contact him through social services.

Gavin had constructed his future self through what he did not have but secretly longed for. He lacked social capital – he did not have the family support systems and structures to foster his interests, to help him build on these and support him in exploring his options and possibilities. Nor, seemingly, were these available to him outside the home. Whereas Gavin had searched for his family to find an identity, Sandra's identity was so closely bound up with that of her family and theirs with hers, that it seemed impossible to separate them.

So far I have contrasted two students who both had a low degree of involvement in the decision-making processes but whose families had either a very strong or very weak engagement. Now I want to contrast two students who were both actively engaged but again whose respective families had differing degrees of involvement.

In Chapter 3, I described Andrew's determination to visit both local and residential colleges before making up his mind which college he intended to apply for, despite the opinions of his teachers and parents. In the end Andrew chose a college where he would live alongside deaf students but mix with hearing students on local college courses. There was a genuine debate between Andrew, his parents and the school, who were all equally involved in the decision-making process; although it would have been interesting to see what would have happened had he chosen to go to a local college.

By contrast Stuart, although equally determined, largely ploughed his own furrow when it came to deciding what to do when school ended. When he was 12 years old Stuart had found himself a job on the market so he understood what work entailed. Home and school saw Stuart in very different lights. His mother described him as 'a very good kid really ... never causes trouble, never gets into fights' whereas the SENCO at his comprehensive school described him as 'immature and light-fingered' and often in trouble. In Year 10 Stuart was given a statement of special educational needs. During his last two terms at school he joined a college link scheme and the school anticipated that he would then follow a pre-vocational course before progressing to a work-based training scheme. But things did not turn out this way and Stuart takes up the story:

> Well, I got messed around so many times at college, I just got fed up with it so I didn't go for it in the end, then I went for a trainee job at Mitsubishi up Mill Lane. I didn't get a reply from there so I went to

Careers and they told me about the warehouse job so I went for that and I got it.

From being monosyllabic Stuart had changed into an articulate and self-confident young man in the space of a few months. He had taken matters into his own hands and found himself a job without the help of his family just as he had done when he was 12 years old.

In summary, the majority of parents generally exercised a high degree of influence on their children and had a direct involvement in the decision-making processes, in some cases to the exclusion of their children. But Kylie and Gavin, with little or no support forthcoming from their families, needed just as much support to enable their voices to be heard as young people like Maria, Costas, Malcolm, Sandra and Kim. The extent to which parents in turn were listened to or helped to be part of the formal decision-making processes is something to which I return in Chapter 5. For now I explore the extent to which the young people's own aspirations and dreams were taken into account in influencing what happened.

Aspirations, strengths and interests: possible and impossible selves?

An aim of careers education programmes is to help young people articulate their aspirations and explore their own strengths and interests. Here are some of the things the young people in this study wanted to do or become:

- Leave school
- Go to college
- Work in a bank
- Work with children
- Join a youth club
- Look after animals
- Have a family
- Live in a big house with a cat and a dog
- Be a van driver's mate
- Become an actor
- Go out with friends
- Become a psychiatrist or a barrister
- Go to the pub with their mother
- Live at home

The list touches on all aspects of their lives – education, training, work, social life, leisure activities, living arrangements and family.

Sometimes how they saw themselves and who they wanted to become was challenged by the nature of their disability. James saw himself as an active and sociable person. He dreamt of becoming a policeman but had recently become reconciled to the fact that this was beyond his physical capacity. His teacher seemed unaware of his struggles in coming to terms with his impairment, its impact on his self-image and consequently his search for an identity. He described movingly how he longed to walk and run like other people.

> ... as I have grown up, I have got more used to being in a wheelchair but I still feel that I would like to get out of this and start walking on my own. Get out of these [callipers] and run off but that is not going to be possible either ... When I was quite young I found that really tough to come to terms with but now I am just getting on with it because I know that I won't ever do what I want because of this wheelchair.

Sometimes a real aptitude or interest in a particular subject area got lost in logistical considerations. An extract from Gavin's annual review serves as a demonstration.

Educational psychologist:	What about drama? You've got an excellent report for drama. Are you not going to do GCSE drama, Gavin?
Gavin:	No.
Teacher:	With the GNVQ it's a double option.

Drama as an option was dismissed. Subsequent discussions between the psychologist and Gavin's teacher revealed that timetable clashes meant that Gavin was prevented from developing what appeared to be a talent and no time was given to exploring how these difficulties might be overcome. Logistical barriers stood in the way of the one opportunity the school might have had to keep Gavin within the school system. Kvaslund (2004) believes that the role of the timetable in school culture acts as a mechanism for ensuring adult security and, as in this case, can actively work against social inclusion. There is just a chance that had Gavin been able to pursue a subject he enjoyed and excelled at he might have remained at school.

Tensions emerged between the pupils' expressed interests and what professionals assumed would be the best, or in most instances the only, route for a pupil to take. Rusteimer describes this in her study of young people with learning difficulties in colleges of further education as 'educational or vocational positioning' (2000: 31). These assumptions are generally based on custom and practice following the routes taken by other students from the same school or college. Sometimes on the face of things, there was often very little real choice available. As Malcolm's teacher put it, 'You can only choose what is there. Things aren't in place for people like Malcolm. I mean you have a very limited choice.'

Nevertheless, it should have been possible to take more account of students' individual aspirations than was the case. For example, Malcolm knew that his inability to read, including reading maps, could constitute a major stumbling block to his becoming a van driver's mate. However, at no point in the annual review meetings was this aspiration ever discussed, although various reports alluded to his enjoyment of manual work and his wish to improve his reading. Had Malcolm's aspirations been taken seriously they could have contributed to the formulation of his transition plan and his curriculum. It is possible then that he would not have dropped out of school.

Overall students' own strengths and interests appeared to play very little part in the decisions that were made about curriculum options and post-school placements, despite the stress on learner involvement in the *Code of Practice* and 'personalized learning' more generally. Broadly speaking personalized learning in mainstream literature and policy has come to mean learners and teachers jointly negotiating individual programmes selected from a menu of possibilities so that they become co-designers in deciding the what, how and where of an individual's programme. Of course this has enormous implications for the organization and structure of mainstream education, and Leadbetter (2004) argues that if personalized learning is to become a reality in education then the 'script' will have to be rewritten to reconceptualize how the curriculum is organized. In Gavin's case his interests would have become the driving force in designing his Year 9 options, not the school timetable.

Most young people can communicate something of their preferences, from their most basic needs to sophisticated ambitions for their adult lives and how they are going to achieve them. Yet most students with learning difficulties and/or disabilities are dependent on others not only to help them realize their ambitions but also, sometimes, to acknowledge that they have such personal interests and aspirations. This in turn affects the extent to which these are taken seriously enough to influence decision-making.

Gender and ethnicity

The extent to which gender and ethnicity (as opposed to class) determine career path has been an on-going debate in the career learning literature. Gender appeared to play some part in the attitudes and consequently the expectations placed on the young people. For example, had Kylie been a boy would she have been expected to take so much responsibility for her younger siblings? Had James been a girl, perhaps his parents would not have stressed the need for him to be as independent as possible, which in turn influenced his commitment to going away to college. And if Sandra had been male, then perhaps her parents would not have felt the same overwhelming need to protect her.

The small amount of research into the experiences of young disabled people from ethnic minorities stresses the importance of recognizing how concepts of adolescence and adulthood vary between cultures. In their study of young people with learning difficulties from a South Asian background Maudslay et al. (2003) challenge the importance placed on independence from the family as a desirable outcome for young people when in many cultures the family maintains responsibility for all its members throughout their lives. They also concluded that staff generally saw young people first as disabled and only second in terms of their ethnicity.

Nasreen's story best illustrated the complex interplay of gender, culture and disability in shaping identity and 'horizons for action'. Her concern about marriage threaded its way through most of our conversations, acting as a recurrent theme. She recalled in her childhood overhearing a conversation between her father and a doctor about her chances of marriage:

> When I was younger my dad was talking to the doctor and I was only about 8 at the time and I can't remember much but he was talking about it because he was talking about marriage and me and asking whether I could get married so basically I don't know what is in store for me

Although she aspired to go to university and then to become a psychologist she saw her family's wish for her to marry as the biggest single obstacle to achieving her ideal lifestyle which was to, 'Live somewhere in quite a big house, in quite a green area where I have access to the city, access to greenery'.

The pressures on her to marry and have a family came not only from her family but from her wider community although she distinguished between religious traditions and cultural expectations:

> For example, with children, the woman is the one who is expected to take care of them, personally I scorn that fact, for example if you are a young mother and you have just got married and had a child, you are the one expected to look after it and give up your job. The husband would not be expected to look after the child, oh no, but personally I think that is ridiculous. Everybody has their own opinions and partly Western influence as well ... People have never said this outright which is that a woman is expected to have a baby as soon as she gets married. These are the expectations, these are not the religious expectations, these are the cultural expectations.

She was also concerned about giving birth to a child who was blind, knowing that there were already five members of her family with this inherited condition. The possibility of having an operation to restore her sight also filled her with alarm, believing that if successful this would increase her chances of marriage. She said, 'I am used to living on my own, I have never had sight, so I never know what I have missed and I am almost going to have to start from the beginning, learning what ... marriage I mean.'

So Nasreen struggled with a number of conflicting pressures on her: her blindness; her family's expectation that she would marry and have children; the fear of having children with glaucoma; and her own career aspirations. Like other young people from ethnic minorities (Morris 1999) she experienced considerable alienation and loneliness when she went on to a residential college since the college was insensitive to her particular cultural traditions. Morris stresses the importance for services to support young people from ethnic minority backgrounds in dealing with issues of identity and racism.

Adolescence and adult status – 'One of the lads'

Having a job remains one of the most powerful indicators of adult status in society today and for Stuart and Malcolm their dreams were, as Malcolm put it, to be 'with the lads'. As described earlier in this chapter, once Stuart got a job he was transformed from school boy to adulthood and employee – he was no longer confronted every day with things he could not do and regarded as 'other', he was now in an environment he understood and felt comfortable in. He had joined the world of work and was already planning his next move. When I asked Malcolm about what he liked about work he said: 'I have a laugh with them [the other men]. Have a laugh and a joke with them. They are alright.' At work with these men he felt accepted and valued and, like Stuart, he felt part of the working world and hence an adult.

But whereas Stuart made a successful transition to work, Malcolm's story illustrates some of the barriers that can be encountered. At weekends he helped his uncle deliver chairs and tables. Although his aim was to be a van driver's mate he was concerned about his inability to read maps and road signs, but his school teachers were not aware of this. Whether or not Malcolm should leave school and get a job was an on-going debate spanning three years. Both he and his mother wanted him to get a job but the school insisted that he must first learn to travel independently, something his father forbade. Meanwhile Malcolm became more and more difficult at home, flying into uncontrollable rages. Malcolm continued to go to school but gradually his attendance dropped off and by his third transition meeting when he was 17 he insisted that he wanted to leave school. His father was not present. This was a tense meeting as the agenda swung back and forth between whether

Malcolm should leave school and whether he should start travelling independently. Here is an example of one exchange:

Mrs Lewis:	I'm not the problem, it's his dad. He can't let him walk to school. He's worried about him. He wraps them up in cottonwool to make him feel better.
Teacher:	Malcolm's probably not being stretched, this is the problem.
Deputy head:	What will happen when Malcolm's 40?
Malcolm:	Yeah!

This small exchange illustrates Malcolm's insights into his problems with his father but this was not followed up. The meeting agreed a plan of action for travelling to school but his father disapproved and soon afterwards Malcolm stopped going to school. By July Malcolm was left doing nothing, as his father and uncle had had a disagreement. Unlike the rest of the family who seemed to ignore their father's anxieties, Malcolm was unable to express his frustrations verbally so he rebelled in the only way he knew and just stopped going to school.

As Mitchell (1999) pointed out in her study of special school leavers open employment, while desirable, is often difficult to achieve particularly for young people with more complex learning difficulties. Paid work was a real option for Malcolm but so many factors got in his way: his father's fears, the failure of everyone to listen to what Malcolm was saying, and finally the inadequacy of the transition review meeting as a forum for dealing with such complex family problems.

Friends

What part did friendships play in influencing the preferences of students? Riddell et al. (2001) observe that the friendship networks of many young people with learning difficulties and disabilities are often restricted to other disabled young people. They remain locked into segregated groupings. This was true of all but one of the nine young people from special schools in this study who appeared to have few or no friends in their local neighbourhoods. For Andrew, David, Nasreen and James concern about social isolation seems to have been one of the contributory factors in their decision to go to specialist residential colleges. Costas, Malcolm and Kim each tried to build a network of friends but were prevented from doing so by their parents. Kim tried to widen her social network by joining a youth club but her attempts as described earlier were blocked by her mother, while Costas was forbidden to give the family telephone number to any of his friends at school. Malcolm had found a group of men at his uncle's work he liked to be with but aside from this group he had no friends of his own age.

Riddell et al. (2001) maintain that people with learning difficulties are most at risk of losing friendships during periods of transition and flux in their lives. A survey of parental attitudes towards transition planning (Raphael 2003) found that many parents felt that the development of social networks was not taken account of during the transition planning process. Similarly a number of parents in this study were concerned about their child's continued access to friendship networks. The fact that Sandra had friends in the local community was one of the reasons why Mrs Harding wanted her to remain living at home. As the father of a deaf child, David's father, Bill Francis, described his concerns over the social isolation of his son:

> *Int:* Does he have friends in the local community?
>
> *Bill:* No, no . . . No one can sign. No, that is the problem. You see when we moved here, we moved here for him to go to that school but we didn't really realize that a lot of the children are boarding there, we thought they lived round in the local area. So we moved here to get him a good social life, but it didn't work out. It got him the school, but he got no social life at all.

This concern over David's social isolation at home prompted his father to persuade the local authority and his school to let David become a weekly boarder. At first the school were reluctant, believing that some of the other pupils who boarded could have a negative effect on David's behaviour but Mr Francis was adamant that 'messing about' with peers is part of growing up: 'He may be silly, but they are silly anyway, so why can't he be silly with people who are, you know, his own peer group.'

What of the young people who went to community schools? All three of them had friends both at school and in their home neighbourhoods whom they spent time with and who seemed to have an important influence on them. One of Kylie's reasons for dropping out of school was that her friends did the same thing. Of the two friends Stuart mentioned one had gone to college while another had got a job. Gavin was described by his foster mother as having 'loads of friends' and Gavin himself thought that his friends would have the most influence on whether he stayed or left school at 16.

It could be argued that it was fear of lack of friendships rather than friendships themselves that was a more important influence on the choice of post-school destinations for a number of these young people. The failure of their schools to recognize the importance of actively fostering friendships as part of link schemes with local mainstream schools was an important influence in helping to shape the attitudes of some of these young people towards integrated provision and hence their decisions to go to specialist colleges. Other people, generally parents, acted as gatekeepers to friendships, either because of transport difficulties arising from distance or fear of letting their child travel independently or because it was just not physically possible.

Sometimes parents failed to understand the importance of friendships but it was also due to the overwhelming complexity of the issues that many of their families had to cope with.

Self-perceptions

How does a young person's disability and/or learning difficulty influence other considerations in the decision-making process? A dilemma faced by four of the students was whether to choose a college on the basis of the courses offered or its type, i.e., whether it was a mainstream or specialist residential college.

The impact of disability on how young disabled people construe themselves has been the subject of a number of studies including Allan (1999) and Rusteimer (2000). Both concluded that young people respond to and deal with their disabilities in different ways. For some students contact with other disabled people is a major factor in making their post-school choices but, for others, the choice of course is also important. David, James, Nasreen and Andrew all faced this dilemma.

Each of them saw themselves as different from non-disabled people and as part of a distinct other group: 'I need a peer group of my own thought [sic]' (Nasreen); 'I want a job with other deaf and not with hearing' (David); 'I wouldn't feel comfortable if I was just on my own [in a mainstream college]' (Andrew). While David, Nasreen and Andrew seemed comfortable with their disability, James was distressed by other people's attitudes to his disability:

James: When I am out in the streets with my mum and dad I feel like I am an alien and that I shouldn't be there, I should be at home.

Int: What makes you feel that?

James: Because when I am going down the street or going in the shopping centre with my mum and dad and my family, people just come past us and stare at us, it just gets so annoying. I mean sometimes it has even stopped me from going out because I haven't liked the feeling that people stare at me. Like, why are they staring at me? Is anything wrong with me? I'm only in a wheelchair and I mean they could be in a wheelchair one day with arthritis or their hip joints playing up or something, you know, and then they will be stared at.

Int: Do you feel you notice it more now than when you were younger?

James: Yes ... Change in me, I suppose, I have become more aware of what is around me as I am older.

Their attitudes towards mainstream colleges were shaped by their participation in link schemes between their special and mainstream schools. James and Nasreen both described the social isolation they had experienced. James said:

> They don't get to see what we are like; they just get to see us for say an hour or two hours so they don't get used to us. Maybe if they came here for a day or so each week that would be better, they could work here and see how we find it. Just see us a little better and get on with us a little bit more. When we go we just work in a small little group . . .

Based on her experiences of mainstream schooling, Nasreen believed that segregated provision meant the best provision as well as the chance to be with others who shared her experience of being blind and who were on, what she described as, 'the same academic level'. Going to a residential college meant increasing her chances of getting into university.

Their preferences were also influenced by social considerations. Andrew wanted the right course but he also wanted to be with deaf *and* hearing students. On the other hand, David believed that being with other deaf students was most important. James preferred to go to a residential college which he thought would make him more independent although he too wanted to go to a college where there were opportunities to mix with non-disabled students. Like many other non-disabled young people, for James the wider experience of living away from home was a more important consideration than his academic programme. As Mitchell says, 'residential college . . . was viewed as a sort of surrogate mode of transition, providing a gradual break with past childhood dependence' (1999: 764).

4.4 Conclusions

To a large extent the influences on young people with learning difficulties or disabilities in making decisions about their future lives are no different from the influences on all young people. The difference lies not so much in the nature of the influences but in how far these influences are acknowledged by others as an integral part of the young person's experience of growing up and deciding what they want to do when they leave school. To ignore individual attributes such as personal interests; preferences and competences; the significance of friends in making post-school choices; the need to assert their adolescence and impending adulthood; the importance of gender and cultural differences; as well as to deny the need to explore individual 'horizons for action', is to maintain differences that are unjustifiable. Indeed, only by recognizing the similarities will the processes be improved.

That is not to say that the influence of the young person's disability or learning difficulty should be ignored but it is here that the nature of the student's special educational need begins to make a difference. The young people I met with sensory and physical disabilities had a strong sense of themselves as disabled and their disability was one of a number of factors which influenced and shaped their ideas and opinions. The title of a radio programme on disability entitled 'No triumph, no tragedy' captures the essence of what I am trying to say. What seemed to be missing in many of the accounts I have described was an understanding of disability in the context of the young people's experience of growing up and thinking about their future as disabled adults. Several of them expressed very clearly their belief in themselves as part of a separate, identifiable group. To disregard the impact of a young person's disability is to ignore an integral part of who they are and how they have shaped their identities or have been shaped. As Liz Crow (2003: 146–7) puts it in her critique of the social model of disability, 'I am arguing for a recognition of the implications of impairment ... Acknowledging our personal experiences of impairment does not in any way disregard the tremendous weight of oppression, nor does it undermine our alignment with other civil rights movements'.

What seemed to be missing was some recognition of the young person's unique, daily experience of difficulties in learning or impairment as an integral part of their experiences of growing up and thinking about their futures. To disregard the impact of their impairment or learning difficulty is to ignore an integral part of who they are and their identities.

Alternatively, to regard their disability as their defining characteristic and the only factor to be taken into consideration is to ignore other equally important aspects of who they are and who they want to become. Instead, like those with learning difficulties that Armstrong (2003) interviewed and the young people from South Asian communities in Maudslay et al.'s (2003) study, the fact of their disability overrode the ordinariness of their aspirations and concerns. The young person's disability came to dominate the thinking of those who were meant to be supporting them. Being 'other' was more important than being the same. It is important to acknowledge however that some young people were proud of their difference – their disability remained an integral part of their identity and who they were. Thus it is not possible to generalize. Their responses differed: some were possibly unaware of their disability, some were proud, some struggled, some were angry and others were confused.

This chapter has also been concerned with the influence *of* young people on the decisions that are to be made, their personal agency. While there was not a clear distinction between those pupils with learning difficulties and those without the former tended to rely more on others to facilitate their participation and contribution to the decision-making processes. The extent to which they were able to assert their preferences and make active choices generally lay in the gift of others. As well as having strong personalities and a clear and largely positive sense of themselves as disabled young people, Nasreen, Andrew and James were free to assert their preferences despite being circumscribed by other considerations and assumptions. Arguably Kylie asserted her choice by dropping out of school as circumstances overwhelmed her, while Maria's mother decided on her behalf with Maria's needs being largely disregarded. The modest aspirations of Costas and Kim went unheeded. So the pupils with learning difficulties were least likely to have their views considered partly due to the failure of others to recognize and respond to their attempts to communicate.

In Chapter 5 the nature of the influences on parents as well as their influence on the process is explored in more depth.

Improving transition planning

1   Contrast the stories of Sandra and Gavin: what different forms of support and intervention might have enabled them to play a more active role in the decisions that were being made?

2   What steps does your organization take to recognize and celebrate the cultural backgrounds of your learners? How are young people from ethnic minorities supported in their transition to adulthood?

3   Jay (2003) describes how Circles of Support can build on friendships to provide a powerful network of on-going support during the transition years. Find out about Circles of Support in your area and how they can support transition planning.

4   Provide opportunities in tutorial sessions for young people to explore how they feel about their impairment or learning difficulty. This could involve the use of role plays, telling stories or painting pictures.

5   Invite past students who have left your school or college to come back to talk about what happened when they left school. Encourage them to send letters, emails or photographs showing what their new life is like.

6   When students make visits to post-school or college options help them to link up with students who they knew at school or college.

5 Listening to parents

5.1 Introduction

The *Special Educational Needs Code of Practice* (DfES 2001) requires that parents participate in the transition planning process. For most of the parents I spoke to this was a period of anxiety rather than of optimism. Of course most parents hope that their children will live safe and happy lives. However, while expressing similar thoughts, the parents in this study also had many fears and dilemmas, exacerbated by the fact that they and their children had few real choices: 'Well, we both want him to be as independent as possible and to have a proper job not sitting in a sheltered workshop-type place' (Mrs Simpson).

Some worried about their children having to leave home, 'I mean, no parent likes their children going away from home, but nevertheless you have to accept it' (Mr Hussein). Others were concerned about bullying and physical or sexual abuse:

> a lot of these colleges I've heard some things about. People that stay at places, they end up being abused ... I know people do get interviews but these people do get attracted to these jobs and if anything like that happened, I'd be extremely upset to say the least.
>
> (Mr Harding)

Yet parents can sometimes be dismissed by professionals as over-protective or, alternatively, as uninterested. Gascoigne (1995: 138), herself a parent of three disabled children, eloquently describes the feelings of many parents as their child approaches the school leaving stage.

> Parents are torn by conflicting wishes for and on behalf of their children as they approach the end of their formal school education and begin to consider the range of future options. On the one hand they want their child to become as independent as possible, and on the other hand they wish to extend their protection of them. This is true of all parents, whether or not their child has special needs. The feelings are exaggerated however where the pupil has special needs. The parents have probably fought many battles both within the home and with external agencies over the years to maximise their

child's independence. The approach of adulthood in their child may be a time when early hopes are finally dashed and/or where the hopes being realised cause an onset of panic.

I have argued that families have a direct as well as indirect influence on decisions taken at 16 and on post-school options in general, whether or not the young person has a learning difficulty or disability. So what is the nature and extent of the influence of the families of children with special educational needs? And are there additional or different factors at work?

There has been relatively little UK research into the experiences and needs of parents of children with learning difficulties and/or disabilities during school leaving, despite evidence to suggest that they find the period surrounding their child's transition from school particularly difficult. *Valuing People* (DoH 2001b) describes the phase as often 'stressful and difficult' for young people and their families while a survey by Heslop et al. (2002) reached similar conclusions. They reported that throughout the school-leaving phase parents' need for information was not recognized, they were insufficiently involved in the transition process and they experienced high levels of anxiety.

Lazarus (1993) argues that one way of alleviating stress is through taking action. According to Lazarus, individuals adopt two broad types of coping strategy: *problem-focused*, in which individuals take actions to alleviate the source of anxiety; and *emotion-focused*, in which individuals attempt to manage the emotions associated with a stressor. Of course, sometimes individuals may adopt both approaches, (dual-focused coping), reinterpreting the problem and taking steps to change or solve the issue they face. Individuals bring with them a variety of resources: problem-solving skills, social networks, personal beliefs and values, health and practical resources such as money or professional training. Lazarus (1993) also emphasizes the importance of seeing coping as a process that takes place over time, which he describes as, 'people's ongoing efforts in thought and action to manage specific demands appraised as taxing or overwhelming' (p. 8).

Studies warn against pathologizing parental stress and anxiety through automatically assuming that they are victims of unfortunate circumstances and events (Heifetz 1980). Others suggest that by emphasizing parents' heroic battles with authority, additional burdens are created for those who adopt alternative approaches (Avis 1985). Kelso et al. (2005) point out that by recognizing that parenting a disabled child can be stressful does not automatically invoke a tragedy model of disability, asserting that 'Vulnerability does not imply pathology' (p. 4). Understanding more about the ways that care givers cope with the impact of stress can provide insights into how best to support families, through enhancing and bolstering their natural resources, alleviating stressors and strengthening families' own capacities to manage (Pell and Cohen 1995).

5.2 Coping with change

In this study most parents adopted combinations of problem- and emotion-focused strategies with first one strategy dominating, then the other.

For example, while acknowledging their anxieties and worries Mr and Mrs Simpson adopted a proactive approach in helping James to decide which course he should follow when he went into the sixth form but were thwarted by a lack of support from professionals: '... Saturday morning [work experience], that is the next step. He ought to start trying different things' (Mr Simpson). Initially put off the idea by James' teachers, Mrs Simpson persisted. However despite a visit from a careers adviser who promised a Saturday morning job nothing materialized.

His parents also wanted to ensure that the course that James was following prepared him for his longer term direction. When James first entered the sixth form both his parents went to a parents' evening to find out more about what James was doing, but they were disappointed.

> I came away confused. It didn't seem to fit with anything I tried to relate him to ... I still didn't understand whether he will end up with any qualifications and if he is we still don't know what it was. They seemed to be working from a syllabus, but we didn't see.
>
> (Mrs Simpson)

So despite their best efforts they were frustrated by the lack of support they received.

Sometimes despite being determined to be proactive and problem-focused, parents feel unable to challenge authority. Mrs Demetrios had heard about a work experience scheme for her son Costas and she was determined to raise the subject at his annual review: 'because I always let him [her husband] do the talking but because he couldn't make it so I thought whatever I have got to say I've got to say it'. The school however suggested that Costas do a one day taster which was not what Mrs Demetrios had in mind at all – she had hoped that he would go on to get a full-time work placement. After the meeting she wished she had been more assertive but despite her resolution to ring the careers officer, she lost her nerve.

As Lazarus (1993) observes, responses to stressors change over time. While at first Bill Francis acknowledged that he felt panic-stricken when he thought about David's future, as time passed he found another way of thinking about the problem. His strategy is emotion-focused as he comes to terms with his feelings about his son's deafness:

> I think that is something I have picked up on over the last year [at university], I have been more aware of, that they themselves see themselves as a community or different. His disability is not a disability to him, I mean he just can't hear. But if you can talk his language he can communicate with you. It has just opened me up to a whole new sort of relationship for people with disabilities ... So I have been looking at it more positively.

Mr and Mrs Doyle also became more positive as time passed and they became less anxious about Kim's need to travel independently. At first they were extremely worried: 'I mean it's a nightmare for us. I mean, they do mention her using public transport virtually unaided. I think not just yet. We have got to get confidence on that, you know'. Gradually Mr Doyle became more reconciled to the idea, admitting that they were more frightened than their daughter was and that they were failing to recognize that Kim was growing up. Mrs Doyle remained unconvinced. At the annual review in the same year the conversation turned to what Kim might do when she left school. At first Mrs Doyle refused to recognize that Kim's inability to travel independently would interfere with her post-school options. But later in the meeting Mrs Doyle again raised the topic of travel, but this time she began to confront her own emotions as well. Very nervously she said:

> The major problem is she's not an independent traveller. It's her fear of escalators. My experience with the King's Cross disaster ... We live in Coalport Lane and I can't let her cross such a busy road – no way. She isn't an independent traveller.

Mrs Doyle had been involved in a disastrous fire on the London Underground when many people lost their lives. Even prior to this disaster, Mr Doyle had also always needed support from his wife before using escalators. So the use of public transport represented a major barrier for both Kim and her parents. Yet, in the course of the meeting, Mrs Doyle began to move towards not only recognizing the problem but asking for help and it was agreed that the community health team would work with the family. In this case the school were able to bolster the Doyles' personal resources by arranging for them to have support from the community learning disabilities team.

How individuals handle stressful periods in their lives and the strategies they adopt can be partly explained by their personalities. In Kelsoe et al.'s (2005) study, 14 out of 26 participants mentioned aspects of their personality as an important coping resource. An individual's physical or mental health may also affect their responses. Mr Lewis's agoraphobia probably contributed to his refusal to let Malcolm travel independently. He recognized the family's dependency on his wife to take control of matters:

> Some days we just look at one another and want to run out and not come back. You know what I mean ... Because what I have been through, I have been through hell and back, with my nerves and that, she [his wife] is the backbone of the family really and sometimes she corrects [me] now and again and I understand.

In the end some parents are overwhelmed with the complexity of their lives and withdraw from any engagement with the transition process. The range of pressures faced by Mrs Long, including the arrest of one son for stealing and begging, the suspension from school of another and the loss of her partner and job, left her with very few resources to support Kylie. In many ways she handed over the responsibility of deciding Kylie's future to Kylie herself.

So many parents have ways of coping that are not necessarily recognized and built on by professionals. In the next section I consider further resources that parents used and that helped to shape their responses. Sensitive and highly skilled interventions which are family-focused and which support the natural resources of parents and carers can and do make a difference to the course of events and thereby improve transition planning processes.

5.3 Influences on responses

Among the many influences on parent's responses were how they saw their role as carers, their personal experiences of education, work and of professionals and, finally, the availability of information.

Role as carer

Most parents expect their role as carer to diminish as their children grow up. In contrast, parents of children with special educational needs often see this responsibility as extending throughout their lives, worrying about what will happen when they die:

> *Int:*　　　In the future do you see yourselves as providing pretty much most of what she receives in school now?
>
> *Mr Harding:*　Yeah, pretty much. That about covers it. 'Cos I mean we are a family. I know the circumstances are a lot different but our son goes to work and comes home everyday, 'til he gets married and leaves. But see, Sandra won't have that either, not at the moment she won't have it because I don't think she can develop that way.

The Hardings had a wide network of informal support, including extended family members, yet these links were not valued by her teachers who rather derided the interdependence which characterized Sandra's relationship with her family.

The changing needs of families across the life span and the impact of these changes on family relationships was also illustrated by the Harding family. While the Hardings reaped the benefits of a supportive extended family, Mrs Harding worried about their parents' increasing dependency, knowing that the responsibility of caring for her elderly relatives would fall mainly on her. But Mr Harding was adamant that they would cope and that Sandra should continue to live at home.

This feeling of 'coping against all the odds' was one shared by a number of respondents:

> If you sit back nothing will happen. That's been our experience of these things, if you go out and look for something it is usually there.
> (Mr. Simpson)

> It's always been up to us to ask, nobody has said that you can have this or that, you have always had to push it, you always have to push.
> (Mrs Bailey)

> If I can do it better than him [the social worker] then I don't want him around.
> (Mrs Constandis)

These parents each felt a strong responsibility to step in when they felt that the services were not fulfilling their responsibilities.

Experiences of education and work

Personal experiences were important in framing both positive and negative attitudes towards future options and the decisions that needed to be made. Bill Francis's ideas were shaped by his university course while Mrs Doyle's experience of the King's Cross fire contributed to her fears about Kim travelling alone on public transport.

Parents' own work also influenced attitudes and ideas. Mr Bailey's work as an electrician provided his son Andrew with useful insights and knowledge of the training required. Kim's father had developed his ideas about supported employment schemes at the local supermarket where he worked. This had had both a positive and a negative impact on him. He had begun to think that such schemes were a good idea: they created real work opportunities and they were a means of educating the general public about people with disabilities.

On the other hand, he was very concerned about the attitudes of the store managers and staff and their low expectations:

> he [the employee] gets support from a chap who comes in and visits him but it is not him who is the problem, it is the people he works with are the problem because they don't understand ... they try to make fun of him which is hurtful and it is lack of education on their part and that is what you get ... it is a worrying scene. He is doing baskets all day long from one end of the store to the other. He could do something else, of course he could ... it is the wrong assumption from Superways' point of view... he could be doing something that would stimulate his brain ... I don't think they respect the job he does.

In trying to understand what to expect, some parents drew on their experiences with their other children. Sometimes this knowledge caused them to question why their child with special educational needs had not been offered similar opportunities such as Mr and Mrs Simpson's request for a Saturday job for James.

So, parents drew on a range of their education and work experiences to shape their opinions and ideas about their child's options. However, one of the most powerful influences was parents' experience of professionals.

Experiences of professionals

Much has been written about the negative opinions that many parents have of professionals (see for example Weatherley 1979; Harry 1992; Sandow 1994; Carpenter 1997; Smart 2004) and in many ways the parents in this study were no exception. The main issue for parents seemed to be one of trust and the feeling that some members of staff were not impartial, their suspicions of officialdom, fear of the consequences of complaining, and the tension experienced by some parents in finding a balance between trust and deference. In general, however, schools and teachers were regarded as supportive and parents' main source of advice:

> I get all my advice from Janet [her son's teacher]. She is great.
>
> (Mrs Bailey)

> You can just walk in ... They are very receptive.
>
> (Mrs Harding)

> You can talk to him [the headteacher] like a friend.
>
> (Mr Hussein)

> If we have any concerns we can go there ... I think they are mar-
> vellous what they do.
>
> (Mr Doyle)

So there was a strong sense of reliance on the school as a source of support
and stability and this may well have contributed to some families wanting
their children to stay at school until age 19. Contact with other support
services such as social services was much patchier and the attitudes of parents
more ambivalent.

Careers advisers (whose roles were later superseded by Connexions personal advisers) also began to play an important role although, again, parental
attitudes towards them were mixed and they were unclear about the service's
roles and responsibilities:

> I am never too clear whether people are working for us or whether
> they are working for the system or ... whether they are representing
> us personally, to push our case, or whether they are just there as an
> arbitrator or somebody to sift out, you know, the good from the bad
> ... I don't know whether there were different agendas going on.
>
> (Mr Simpson)

Mrs Constandis was also suspicious of decisions made at official meetings: 'I
don't know that what we say at the review is going to happen anyway. I don't
think things get carried through, it just depends. I think it depends on what
they have available at the time.'

Other parents exhibited a mixture of trust and deference in their relationships with professionals. Harry (1992) identified a similar tension in her
work in the United States with mothers from Puerto Rico of children with
special educational needs and she attributes such feelings of deference to the
cultural background of the mothers. This could help to explain the apparently
contradictory responses of both Mrs Demetrios and Mr Hussein. Despite her
criticisms of the school, Mrs Demetrios experienced difficulties in speaking
out in meetings, particularly in front of the headteacher (a man), always
saying in the end, 'They [the teachers] know best'. Mr Hussein was full of
praise for the school: 'school is tremendous. It gives me hope; I couldn't live
without the school. And the staff at the school are absolutely marvellous'. Yet
he also felt disempowered by the headteacher when he queried the funding
for a residential placement:

> *Mr Hussein:* ... they said they could not discuss it at the time, but if the
> finance did not go through they have got other options.

Int:	How did you feel about that?
Mr Hussein:	Not very good because I would rather know what they can do next ...
Int:	Would you feel able to challenge them about that?
Mr Hussein:	No, I didn't because he [the headteacher] said it wasn't appropriate.

Despite Mr Hussein wanting to know more, he did not feel able to press the headteacher for further information. Access to information plays an important role in increasing parental power and influence within the decision-making process. Yet even when information and advice was made available, parental attitudes towards professionals influenced the trust they placed in the information they received.

Access to information and communication

Access to information is essential if parents are to participate in the decision-making processes. But before you can ask for information you need to know what you don't know. At first, many parents in the study found it difficult to articulate what information they wanted: 'People say, we should ask these things but you don't know to ask anything, do you? I didn't ask it because I didn't know there was any reason to ask' (Mrs Bailey).

In addition to needing to know what questions to ask, parents' information needs fell into six broad categories:

- procedural information, i.e., how decisions would be made;
- understanding the roles and responsibilities of the different services;
- accurate and comprehensive information about post-school options, such as colleges and training schemes, and the types of programmes they offered, as well as employment options;
- practical information about benefits or equipment;
- long-term options and support, such as university entrance or support for their children after they died;
- information and guidance on helping their child deal with sexuality and life-span issues.

Sources of information fell into two main types: official information, received through formal channels such as parents' evenings, school visits, school newsletters, voluntary organizations, official letters and forms, and informal information, often gleaned through chance encounters.

Most parents saw the school as their main source of official information, although sometimes attitudes changed in the light of experience: 'The school said that they were looking into some others for us but they were pretty useless ... they didn't offer us anything' (Mrs Harding).

A common difficulty encountered by many parents is the language used in official documents and meetings. Sometimes they did not understand certain terms, e.g., attainment levels, GNVQ, etc., or they found the language alienating, such as that used in college prospectuses. Parents were upset by terms used as a matter of course by some services, such as 'handicapped' or 'registered deaf'.

Informal sources of information included:

- family friends and neighbours;
- other parents and pupils; and
- the media.

Often, this kind of information tended to confirm rather than challenge already formulated views. In one case a leaflet dropped through a neighbour's door about a local college open day provided exactly the information that Sandra and her family had been searching for in the previous three years. Relying on chance events to gain information was to all intents and purposes exactly what the *Code of Practice* had been set up to avoid. Eight sets of parents cited other parents or children at the same school as sources of information. It is likely that other parents were perceived as more trustworthy than official sources and this seems to be borne out by parents' request for someone impartial to talk to on a one to one basis.

The media was also an important source of information. Mrs Harding described how she and her husband's opinions of residential colleges were confirmed by a television programme:

> Chris and I were watching it [television] and we didn't talk – we just looked, and I can't bear the thought that she would be taken away and something awful would happen to her. Some of these residential homes are quite frightening ... I hate the thought of anything hurting her and we couldn't be there to protect her.

Coupled with the absence of many of the traditional markers associated with growing up and leaving school, the available options were often unclear, as were the procedures associated with planning the next stage. A lack of clear and reliable information only added to parents' sense of powerlessness and consequent anxiety.

5.4 Conclusions

This chapter has focused on the influence and experiences of parents during the lead up to their child leaving school. A number of the young people in the study expressed their confusion and unhappiness as they felt torn between the views and wishes of their parents, what they themselves wanted and the opinions of their school, 'Going round in circles' as one student described it. Parents cope with their feelings in different ways but these strategies were rarely recognized or supported by the professionals with whom they came into contact. Instead parents were generally regarded as overprotective of their child, overanxious, interfering or, alternatively, uninterested. On the whole professionals did not attempt to recast or reframe parents' attitudes to try to see their behaviour in a more positive light, which in turn may have helped to alleviate parental sources of distress and bolster their personal resources.

There were some examples of sensitive and skillfull interventions on the part of professionals in responding to parental anxieties but what is also clear is that some parents who wanted to be more proactive and problem-focused were not supported in doing so, while others who tried to do so became frustrated or disillusioned. Others were uncertain about their role in the transition planning processes and how far they should get involved. It is also clear that the information which might have given them more control over the process and consequently a more equal role was generally not forthcoming. Instead they relied on informal sources of information and support such as family, friends and neighbours.

Examples of good practice in transition planning that foster parental participation are emerging (Heslop et al. 2002) and there are also a number of web-based sources of information (see for example www.myfuturechoices. org.uk). The development of an advocacy and support service 25 years after the Warnock Report (1978) first suggested it, in the form of the Connexions Service, has already shown its worth despite some problems in practice (Rowland-Crosby et al. 2004).

More fundamentally, recent policy initiatives such as Children's Trusts, the National Service Framework and The Children Act 2004 are supporting services to develop what have become known as 'wrap-around services', where the young person and the family lie at the heart of service provisions. This in turn should enable professionals to become more sensitive to what family systems theorists such as Pell and Cohen (1995) and Beckman (1996) describe as families' own capacities to cope with change and stress. The families' own resources need to be built on in concert with official or formal systems. The family support movement, which emphasizes that the overwhelming majority of families have the strength and capacity to change and grow, has begun to influence the development of early intervention and mental health services in the UK (Mental Health Foundation 2002). Circles of Support (Jay 2003) offer a further example of family and community led approaches. Through recasting or reframing parents' attitudes or behaviour in a more positive light and by building on parents' naturally occurring and informal sources of support, professionals can begin to respond more sensitively to the needs of parents, matching their responses to the ways in which parents perceive and cope with transition. This in turn should lead to better transition planning both for and with young people.

Improving transition planning

1   Divide into two groups. One group should adopt the parental perspective and the other the perspective of professionals. On a flip chart spend 10 to 15 minutes brainstorming all the things that you would like to say to each other from your particular perspective about the transition planning process. Then present your ideas to each other.
      After each group has had its say spend some time debriefing and reflecting on the things you might do to improve the support and information that is offered to parents.

2   Invite a local parents' group to talk to you about how best to support parents and carers. You can contact them through your local parent partnership scheme at www.parentpartnership.org.uk

3   Provide parents with a list of questions that they might find useful to ask at different points in the transition planning process.

4   Review all the information that your organization/service produces to decide whether it is free from jargon. The Plain English Campaign provides useful guides on how to ensure that written information is accessible (www.plainenglish.co.uk).

5   Set up a network of parents whose children have already left school or college who would be prepared to offer advice and information to other parents. This could be as simple as a list of telephone numbers or email addresses.

6   Provide information about the transition planning processes and procedures as well as post-school/college options and sources of advice and information.

7   Organize visits to post-school/college options for parents.

8   Make sure that the Connexions personal adviser has made contact with the family and explains their role before the first transition planning meeting in Year 9.

9   Make sure that hard copies of information for parents is available as well as relevant internet addresses.

10 Read the list of information on page 73 that parents said that they

wanted. How does your organization make this information available? Are there any areas where improvements could be made? Check what information the parents and carers of the young people with whom you work would like.

6 Professionals, policies and procedures

6.1 Introduction

In this chapter I discuss how the professionals who worked with the young people and their families exercised their influence through the formal decision-making procedures. I have already described the decision-making 'unit' as having a central core that consisted of the young person and their parents or carers and then an outer and more fluid network of mainly professionals who often changed year to year, such as class teachers and learning support staff. Sometimes personnel changed as responsibility shifted from child to adult services. These professionals had different levels of involvement with the young people and their families as well as different perceptions of their needs and variable degrees of influence.

The 2001 *Code of Practice on the Identification and Assessment of Special Educational Needs* lays down the approach which LEAs and schools should adopt in planning transitional programmes and is described in more detail in Chapter 2. One of the main purposes of the transition planning process is to support young people and their families in making choices about their post-school destinations and to formulate an action plan setting out the support required in the medium- to long-term. Heslop et al. (2002) found that one in five young people did not have a transition plan with many professionals failing to implement the Code's guidance on transition planning. For their part professionals can find themselves torn between the policies and legislation that guide how they work, the demands made on them by students, parents and other colleagues and the need to make their jobs manageable.

What does the *Code of Practice* say about how young people, their parents and professionals should work together? Parents must be invited to all statement review meetings which, from Year 9 onwards, include the transition planning meetings. After the meeting the transition plan must be circulated to parents. Young people do not necessarily have to attend the meetings but they should be fully involved in contributing to any plans that are drawn up. More generally, schools are encouraged by the Code to work in 'partnership' with parents but as Sandow (1994) and Armstrong (1995), among others, have pointed out, the concept of partnership is ambiguous, with comforting connotations but open to multiple interpretations and meanings. The Code suggests that schools need to find out how parents prefer to work with schools (DfES 2001: 26). Working in this way demands an in-depth knowledge of the dynamics of the family and their personal preferences and suggests a more flexible approach to accommodating the changing needs of individual parents and young people. So, for example, partnership working could mean enabling parents to organize work experience for their son or daughter (Mr and Mrs Simpson), holding meetings in the family home to encourage parents to feel more at ease (Mrs Long) or involving inter-disciplinary teams to provide family therapy (Mr and Mrs Lewis).

Which professionals are likely to be involved? The *Code of Practice* suggests that young people and their families are likely to require holistic support from a range of services during the transition process. However the two services that are legally bound to have some involvement with all statemented pupils are the Connexions and social services, both of which continue to struggle to meet the Code's expectations. Others who might be involved include healthcare professionals, further education college staff, LEA officers or educational psychologists.

The implementation of new policies and procedures depends on the willingness of practitioners to accept their new responsibilities and how they choose to interpret the procedures. This can lead to significant variations in practice. Policies are, according to Ozga (2000: 2): 'a process rather than a product, involving negotiation, contestation or struggle between different groups who may lie outside the formal machinery of official policy making'. This definition suggests a complex, dynamic and fluid approach to the question of policy development and implementation.

To ensure that legislation is enacted, checks and balances can be put in place through inspections or audits. Since the transition planning guidance is not enshrined in law and local authorities only have to 'have regard' to its proposals, local authorities and schools have so far had considerable freedom in how they choose to interpret the Code. Furthermore, because the enact-ment of the guidance spans not only phases but disciplines, checking the quality of the overall process is complex. However with the introduction of Children's Trusts and the National Service Framework it is likely that joint Ofsted and social services inspections on the effectiveness of transition planning arrangements spanning phases and services will be conducted.

Ball's (1994) and Ozga's (2000) approaches to policy implementation remind us that individuals bring their own personal circumstances and per-spectives to bear on how they interpret new policies. Policies are not intro-duced into a vacuum. In some cases, of course, practice precedes policy and professionals have already developed their own ideas and beliefs about what makes for effective practice. Many of the practitioners I spoke to had a real commitment to the needs of the students and their families, and were sometimes faced with genuine dilemmas about the best course of action to take. Their responses to the *Code of Practice* guidance on transition planning could be grouped as follows:

- Making minor changes to practice, but generally continuing to rely on custom and practice.
- Going through the motions of the new procedures and processes but without challenging their underlying assumptions.
- Reviewing previous practice with a view to challenging underlying assumptions and making changes in line with new guidelines where necessary.

6.2 Responses to transition policies and procedures

Custom and practice

Some professionals continued to rely on custom and practice in guiding what they did, without questioning their practice. Assumptions continued to be made about what was 'best' for the young person. Here I discuss two aspects of practice: the timing of the first transitional reviews and discussions about leaving, and staff assumptions about the destinations of young people when they reach 16.

Timing

The Code recommends that the first transition planning meeting should take place in Year 9. Yet some parents of pupils at special schools said that, even though their child was only two or three years off the statutory school-leaving age, teachers and other professionals were reluctant to discuss the subject of school leaving with them:

> I asked to see someone about careers a couple of years ago, because I was that worried about what he could do and she more or less said come back when he is a little older. I can't do anything yet. It seems to be the ongoing thing, you know, we will look at it soon but not just yet.
>
> (Mrs Simpson)

Delaying discussions about post-school options may act as a means of regulating demands on staff time, or alternatively, as a way of protecting parents and pupils from undue anxiety. Most of the special schools, for their part, assumed that all their pupils would stay at school until they were 18 or 19. They also assumed wrongly that the parents were aware of their sixth forms' existence, as illustrated by the following exchange:

Mrs Simpson:	When do we talk about what James is going to do in the sixth form?
Deputy head:	Have you visited it? I wish we had a leaflet about it.
Mrs Simpson:	No – I don't know anything about the sixth form.

School policy, in this instance, was based on custom and practice rather than the guidance in the Code or the needs of young people or their parents.

Opportunities to think about and discuss the future were also regulated by the timing of the first transition planning meeting. Although the Code recommends that the first meeting should be held when the pupil is in Year 9, along with the statutory review of the statement, the schools exercised a good deal of flexibility in how they interpreted this guidance. While at Gavin's comprehensive school the staff used the Year 9 annual review to agree Key Stage 4 options alongside considering future destinations, other schools waited until Years 10 or even 11 before discussing options and post-16 destinations. This was particularly so where, as described above, the school had an attached sixth form or where at 16 pupils traditionally moved on to residential specialist colleges. It is to assumptions made about post-school destinations that I now turn.

Destinations

The Code recommends that the school and the Connexions personal advisers should provide guidance on post-16 options and that parents and pupils should 'have their views listened to and recorded separately and with respect for any differences of opinion' (DfES 2001: 30). In practice the staff tended to make assumptions about their pupils' destinations at 16+, generally assuming that special school pupils would progress to the school sixth form or residential college and that mainstream pupils would move on to the local college. Once there, colleges assumed that after finishing a link course students would automatically progress on to certain pre-vocational and work-based training programmes. This pattern matches earlier research by Ward et al. (1991) and Mitchell (1999) in which post-school destinations were largely determined by the type of school the young people attended. In other words they are 'educationally and vocationally positioned' (Rusteimer 2000). Consequently, pupils experience a further restriction of what is already a fairly limited set of options and choices as a result of staff attitudes.

Occasionally students or parents challenged these assumptions. Each of the three special schools for pupils with sensory or physical disabilities assumed that most of their pupils would go to residential colleges. Although Andrew eventually decided to go to a residential college he discovered the existence of local colleges during my interview with him, and he insisted on visiting them. A note was added to his transition plan, 'An addition to the review to read that Andrew will be considering both mainstream and specialist colleges'.

Sandra's parents also challenged the school's assumption that their daughter would go to a residential college but the cost of their disagreement meant that, three years later and two months before Sandra was due to leave school, nothing had been agreed. They eventually found some local provision with the help of a neighbour. Why was it so difficult for Mr and Mrs Harding to challenge the prevailing orthodoxy? Mrs Harding's explanation was as follows:

> it didn't seem that the school knew anything about this college and what we were asking for. They had plenty of residential homes, loads of them, and it seems that we were a bit of a pain in the neck because we were a bit out of the norm ... and they take it all over and because we wanted to keep her in our area ... we would have liked to have known about a year ago of all the colleges that are in our area so that we could have had a lot to go to and have a look at. They did offer us to go and have a look at residential ones as I said, but that is what we weren't interested in, we didn't want that.

The underlying explanations for these attitudes are complex. Perhaps professionals were maintaining control through restricting the amount of information that was passed to parents and young people. An alternative explanation could be that professionals are anxious to maximize the time young people remain in education before having to cope with the uncertainty of the labour market and adult life:

> I think they need to be taken quite gently into life after St. Peter's [rather] than having to face it abruptly this year. I very much hope that she will stay on into the sixth form. I think it would be a tragedy if she left school early so I suppose one of the things to ascertain is that she is going to stay in the sixth form.
>
> (Teacher)

Professionals were in effect extending the transition period. As Sam Smiley, a Year 10 teacher at Marchmount School explained: 'You can only choose what is there. Things aren't in place for people like Malcolm. I mean you have a very limited choice and I think that is the reality'. Like the teachers of Kylie and Gavin, Sam was afraid that once Malcolm left the education system he would slip through the network of support. It is significant that all three pupils eventually dropped out of school of their own accord and seemed destined to become excluded from the mainstream of society.

An additional barrier to students attending local provision is patchy access to health care. If a student attends a residential college then therapeutic services are more readily available than in a sector college. In the past local provision has been much harder to organize, particularly where students have to move between health trusts. There are signs of improvement as healthcare services are reorganized and systems begin to be put into place that support interagency working.

In this section I have argued that, despite the introduction of the Code's guidance on transition planning, with its emphasis on participation, options and choice at 16, many professionals continue to rely on custom and practice to guide their responses. By delaying discussions about post-school options or by making assumptions about the next steps for their pupils the need for staff to engage in having to support students and parents in making decisions was nullified. The corollary of this approach is that there is then no need to begin discussions about post-school options in Year 9 because destinations are already clear. However, this wish to delay discussions can also arise from staff's own anxieties about the future of their pupils and their own lack of confidence in helping parents deal with the uncertainty of the future.

Going through the motions

Another way of coping with policy changes is to make the new procedures fit existing practices and to 'go through the motions' rather than undertaking the kind of wholesale review of values and working practices that may be implied. One of the Code's major procedural innovations was the introduction of transition planning from Year 9 onwards as part of the regular annual review process.

The Code provides guidance on who is to be invited to the meeting, their responsibilities and the purpose of the transition plan. In practice however schools found it difficult to reconcile the dual purposes of the meetings, i.e., reviewing the statement and discussing the transition plan. In many of the 18 meetings observed, the majority of time was spent reviewing the statement rather than discussing transitional issues:

> To be honest with you, I don't know if I am doing the job right, I don't know what I should be doing in a way. I am not quite sure what the perfect chair of an annual review should do ... I suppose I like to develop an atmosphere of informality in the hope that people will feel able to contribute as and when they would like to. I am very aware of trying to lead people through a few documents making sure that everybody understood them and that everybody has agreed with what has been written.
>
> (Ann James)

One of the problems for those managing the meetings was the multiple agendas that individuals brought with them. Using a questionnaire, participants were asked to compare what they hoped would be achieved and then what they thought was actually decided at the meetings. In the following discussion 'short-term' is used to mean within the next 12 months, 'medium-term' to denote the next step on leaving school and 'long-term' meaning any time thereafter.

Those teachers who responded (14 teachers, heads and deputies) saw the meetings as an opportunity to review pupil progress and the pupil's statement and to agree short-term targets. However, a few (five) also saw these occasions as an opportunity to pass on information to parents about the curriculum their child would be following and about procedures for choosing post-school placements. In general then, the emphasis was mainly on the curriculum and the immediate future. In contrast, the four careers advisers (personal advisers) were each more concerned with exploring the student's medium- or longer term plans, as was the occupational therapist. Parental expectations were mixed, with most of them wanting more information about their child's progress, the curriculum and post-school options or procedures.

Respondents were also asked to comment on what they thought the meetings had achieved. This highlighted some important tensions between parents and professionals. Just under half the parents (5 out of 11) expressed disappointment with the outcomes as opposed to one-eighth of the professionals (3 out of a possible 24). Parents used phrases such as 'disappointed', 'very vague', 'no change, no decisions' to describe their feelings. Sometimes these differences of perspective, particularly between parents and professionals, led to anger and frustration. For instance Bill Francis had gone to David's review expecting to find out which residential college his son might attend and how the place would be funded. He saw no point in discussing local provision. On the other hand the professionals at the meeting all felt that the purpose of this particular review was only to begin to explore post-16 possibilities including local opportunities. The careers adviser wrote:

> I would not expect any decisions to be made as I do not feel this is the appropriate venue for making decisions but an opportunity to highlight issues which need further discussion and subsequently decisions. The review is one part of the decision-making process.

There were also tensions between professionals. An occupational therapist commenting on the focus on short-term rather than longer term planning noted, 'The reviews are not fulfilling a useful purpose'. Maria's teacher and her learning support assistant both resented the dominance of the social worker's agenda at Maria's annual review meeting, feeling that no one else had a chance to contribute.

Some schools found the dual purposes of the Year 9 and subsequent reviews difficult to manage. They continued to focus on reviewing the statement and setting short-term educational targets, paying little attention to medium- or longer term planning, particularly where they assumed that the young person would remain in the same school until they were 19. It was not until the penultimate or final reviews that much attention was paid to transitional issues.

Questioning or reviewing current practice

While the majority of staff showed little awareness of the different expectations of participants and the impact that these were likely to have on the conduct of meetings, others questioned their value in supporting the transition process. Sometimes meetings touched on difficult or sensitive issues, which were opened up for discussion but then avoided. Two teachers expressed their concerns about this. Lucy Smith, Gavin's support teacher, questioned the value of some annual reviews, believing that most did little more than offer a formal recognition of the statement review. Mel Grant, a teacher at Marchmount School, agreed. After one of Kim's reviews he shared his concerns that Mr and Mrs Doyle felt unhappy with the school but that such meetings did not allow conflicts to emerge, despite the fact that everyone was given an opportunity to speak.

I observed each of Kim's annual reviews and these were largely taken up with the issue of whether Kim should be allowed to travel independently. This was a complex problem for everyone to cope with, including her teachers and her parents. Mrs Doyle raised the problem at Kim's Year 12 meeting and referred to her own experiences in the Kings Cross fire. The response was:

Careers adviser: Is it something she can work on? A little bit at first, find a safe place to cross just in the immediate area. Next year she's going to college on her own. By the time she leaves school she will have to travel if she's to work. Even college progression to the next level course expects them to travel independently.

Deputy head: I think we're jumping too far ahead. We're working on other things.

While the careers adviser was concerned with the longer term, the deputy headteacher, who was chairing the meeting, seemed reluctant to open up the discussion about the family's reluctance to give Kim more independence and Kim's future prospects. However Mel, Kim's teacher, reopened the discussion almost immediately.

Mel:	We've referred Kim to the Community health team – its an interdisciplinary team. They will work with you all.
Mrs Doyle:	When she's due to go out she tells me a few days beforehand. I know she's very nervy. We try to overcome it.
Mr Doyle:	They will advise us as well. We don't know how to approach it.
Mel:	The psychiatrist says it's a very difficult problem. She warned me not to be too teacherly. She wants to focus on what she's achieved.
Deputy head:	Next year what college courses will you do?

Again the deputy head changes the subject and this time succeeds in redirecting the course of the meeting back to more prosaic matters.

Despite his misgivings about the value of some transition planning meetings, Mel was also the most enthusiastic teacher about the Code's guidance on transition. He believed the meetings helped to validate his role as the school leaver's teacher so that, using Ball's (1994) definition of policy implementation, Mel's interpretation of the Code's guidance fitted with his personal beliefs, experiences, skills and context. In other words, the Code had confirmed how he believed he should be working. The local authority had provided some training on different models of transition meetings which he believed should be the 'pinnacle' of their work, for it was at these meetings that professionals, parents and young people could all meet face to face and listen to one another's opinions. He believed that, for parents, the most important aspect of the meetings was the process, whereas for professionals it was the production of completed forms. This was borne out by my own observations of meetings, in which the completion of forms seemed to take precedence over the exploration of issues, as illustrated above. Mel also felt that such meetings should give young people a voice, providing an opportunity for them to tell their parents what they wanted to do. Finally, he saw the meetings as a rite of passage, particularly when a child had attended the school for many years. They were a way of recognizing that a fundamental change was about to take place in the life of the young person and their family and the meeting allowed everyone to share their feelings and emotions about the separation from the school that they were confronting.

Over the course of the three years of this project staff began to question some of their underlying assumptions. At St Peter's School attitudes of staff began to change, perhaps due to new guidance issued by the local authority or an interim project report that I had prepared at their request, or a combination of the two. In any case the deputy head, acknowledging the helpfulness of my report, said he felt discussions with young people and their parents should start sooner rather than later and that, while no definite decisions about post-school destinations were being made in Year 9, such meetings were an opportunity to begin to share information. How far his change of attitude influenced the school's subsequent practice was outside the scope of this particular project.

The outcomes of transition planning meetings should be recorded on a proforma and then used to inform the student's programme of work throughout the next and subsequent years but doubts were expressed by some staff about the effectiveness of these plans. Freda at Marchmount School admitted to never having looked at the forms, but Sue Stapleton at St Peter's reflected on the inadequacies of their current practice:

> For everybody it [transition planning] ought to start earlier, so that we can actually be thinking much more clearly about what's going to happen. The implications if you make this choice. For instance, if you make a choice to go to a mainstream college placement you have then got to sort your own therapy out and all those things. It's very late on in the day for Year 12 to suddenly be facing parents and students with the implications of what choices are going to be. We ought to do it much earlier. I don't think it would have a big impact on the curriculum for Key Stage 4, but I think what we would get is better thinking about what's needed in the sixth form.

It is clear from this statement that Sue and her colleagues were rethinking, not only the relationship between the statement review and transition planning, but also the organizational and curricular implications for the school of offering genuine options to students from Year 9, rather than making assumptions about their progression routes at age 16. So, while there was certainly some evidence to suggest that professionals were clinging to their traditional ways of working and reconceptualizing the Code's intentions by 'domesticating' or 'ritualizing' the new procedures, it was also clear that others were questioning their current ways of working.

It is not easy for staff to challenge the prevailing status quo, however. Exploring Costas' story from the perspective of his teacher, Sam, illustrates just how difficult it was. Sam agreed with Mr and Mrs Demetrios that Costas was probably not in the right kind of provision for him. He felt that Costas would have managed in a mainstream secondary school had he been given sufficient support and thought that he should probably move into a mainstream setting at 16. Sam perceived employers and other education and training providers as holding negative attitudes towards pupils from special schools, often failing to see pupils' potential:

> I don't think we think about those things enough really in a sense, because I have always thought, this is just a personal view, this kid is going to leave school, it would be best for him if he left from a big

> school rather than a special school. In his personal file or his history
> he is not leaving from a special school ... I think this gives a different
> sort of feel when you ask ...

Sam went on to describe how he felt their local college also labelled those
pupils leaving special schools by assuming that they would join separate,
rather than mainstream, link programmes and from there continue on to
specially designed full-time courses. He considered that students leaving his
school were consigned to the conveyor belt of special programmes, even
while knowing, for instance, that Costas was capable of more. 'They tend to
put them into a slot.' Here then, Sam was concerned that college staff did
much the same as some school staff by narrowing options and choices based
on assumptions. Yet none of these ideas were shared at the review meetings or
recorded, and, at his Year 11 review, the deputy headteacher said that it
would be better if Costas stayed at school, so that 'we can keep an eye on
him'. It was also clear that his Year 11 teacher did not share Sam's view of
Costas' capabilities.

> One of the things that I find in the classroom in school and at college
> is that he finds it very difficult to behave appropriately in situations.
> So it's part of social experience of how you cope with being in the
> canteen not just sort of messing about ... these social things are very
> important for Costas to learn this year.

6.3   Conclusions

The influence of professionals was exercised not only through their perceptions of the young people and their families' needs but also through their
responses to and interpretation of policies and procedures, which were
inextricably linked to their personal agendas. Three types of response by
professionals to the Code's guidance were identified: no changes to the ways
in which they worked, continuing to rely on custom and practice; a
'domestication' or accommodation of the procedures, but without challenging underlying assumptions; a questioning of previous practice with a view
to making changes in line with the Code's guidance.

The original concept of a transition planning meeting linked to the
annual review of the statement is located in a medical model of disability.
Professionals meet to discuss the progress of a particular individual and plan
what needs to be done next. Gradually this approach has been modified so
that by now it is common practice for young people and their families to be
involved. The review of the statement is in many ways a different process
from transition planning, which can make the meetings difficult to manage.

An additional problem arises when the approach adopted in the meeting is dominated by professionals and the completion of forms. For all the attempts to put the young person in the driving seat, these formal meetings may not be the best way of involving young people in planning their own futures. The more fluid and person-centred approaches adopted by Circles of Friends, for example, enable young people and their parents to feel more relaxed and able to contribute. An example of how these ideas have been used in practice to open up transition planning meetings is described by Carnaby et al. (2003). Meetings are held in environments familiar to the students; students bring visual aids with them to illustrate their likes and dislikes and they can bring friends into the meeting. Separate meetings are held to discuss health issues at which the student is not present. Most important of all, considerable work takes place using a range of different activities to prepare young people for the meeting.

In listening and talking to the professionals in this study I was struck by their lack of awareness of the power that they wielded, and yet how relatively powerless many parents and young people were in the process. This power flowed partly from the status attached to their roles as teacher, social worker, therapist, etc., but also from the systems within which they operated. Laragy (2004) argues that young people and their families are not equipped with the skills and information that they need to negotiate with services during the transition planning process. The introduction of the Connexions Service has gone someway to providing young people and their parents with a neutral voice and someone to speak on their behalf when needed. The Connexions Service personal adviser is also in the position to provide the continuity between school and post-school provision and between child and adult services. In the final chapter I consider how the different professionals and the systems within which they work can support the transition planning process more effectively.

Improving transition planning

1   Think about a transition planning meeting that you have recently attended. Evaluate the meeting against the following criteria:
    - Importance – how important was the meeting?
    - Membership – were the right people present?
    - Task – did everyone have a shared understanding of the meeting's purpose?
    - Climate – did the atmosphere of the meeting obstruct or support the conduct of the meeting?
    - Openness – were people able to speak their minds or did they feel guarded?
    - Next steps – were the actions arising from the meeting clear?

Invite a colleague to evaluate a meeting that you are running. After the meeting discuss their observations and decide what steps could be taken to improve the conduct of transition planning meetings.

2   Find out about person-centred planning techniques and adapt them for use in your organization (see, for example, www.sandersonassociates.co.uk). For example, you can build sessions into the Careers Education and Guidance programme that enable young people to explore their dreams and aspirations. These can be represented graphically and show not only the young person's dreams but their fears as well and who or what can support them in the future. The creation of each map or picture can involve contributions from everyone in the group saying what they like or admire about the person. These plans can be taken to transition planning meetings and be used as the basis for discussion.

7   How to improve transition planning

7.1   Introduction

The focus of this final chapter is on ways of supporting the transition process for young people aged 14–25. Having a transition plan is helpful but it is the quality of the experiences that support the plan's development and implementation that are more important in the long-term and which will enhance young people's quality of life. In this chapter I discuss the place of the curriculum, personalized learning and interagency working in supporting young people's transition to adulthood. I begin by reflecting on the nature of the curriculum for the transition years.

To date there has been a distinct separation between pre- and post-16 curricula. Pre-16 most students follow a broadly similar curriculum and work towards similar qualifications. Post-16 provision is diverse and characterized by choice and many different qualifications. Most pre-16 students with special educational needs, like their peers, follow a broadly common curriculum which has become increasingly inclusive (Byers et al. 2002). They may or may not undertake examinations at age 16. However while some groups of learners with special educational needs have benefited from improved access to both vocational and academic routes through, for instance, examination accommodations and specialist equipment, others are marginalized by the academic school culture which forces them to leave school at age 16 or earlier. Post-16 the curriculum is generally determined by their destination, which in turn is strongly influenced by the type of school they attended, whether special or mainstream. Post-school destinations include further education, work-based training, specialist residential colleges, employment or, for a few, university. Exact figures are not known, but generally speaking young people with special educational needs attending mainstream schools are likely to leave at age 16 or earlier, while those attending special schools are more likely to stay on (apart from pupils with emotional and behavioural difficulties). Young people with severe or profound and complex learning difficulties may remain beyond age 19 (Florian et al. 2000) with the knock on effect that some will remain in full-time education up to the age of 25.

Recent curriculum thinking (DfES 2004b), described in Chapter 2, has attempted to reconfigure the 14–19 curriculum, seeing it as a seamless offer from which individual learners negotiate and select programmes designed to meet their particular goals and aspirations, spanning schools, colleges and work-based training. To some extent mainstream ideas are therefore catching up with the policy that has already existed in special education for a number of years. This guidance already emphasizes the need to tailor 14+ programmes and the curriculum to match the aspirations of the transition plan. In practice there is still a long way to go, but if the 14–19 curriculum is to be driven by the aspirations and goals of all learners this may benefit everyone. Such an intention will require radical changes in how schools, including special schools, and colleges relate to one another, not least in the levels of trust between them and in how they organize and structure the curriculum.

Despite attempts to rationalize structures across the 14–19 pathways, debates continue over the underlying purpose of the curriculum, particularly for those young people who are working at the earliest stages of the national curriculum or below Level 1 of the Framework for Achievement. On the whole, UK writing on the curriculum tends to reiterate principles rather than providing an exploration of the effectiveness of programmes, so it remains difficult to judge the success of different approaches. On the one hand there is pressure to maintain the focus on improving levels of literacy and numeracy (DfES 2005) implying a functional approach, while on the other there is increasing interest in the social nature of learning and the role of the curriculum in fostering citizenship (QCA 2001, 2004). These different pressures are partly due to differing ideas about the nature of adolescence and transition.

I described different models of adolescence and adulthood and their implications for how we think about the transition phase in Chapter 1. These models were phase-related, agency-related and time-related. How have these ideas influenced transition planning and the transition curriculum?

Phase-related curriculum models emphasize the role of the curriculum in preparing young people for adult life. The curriculum is largely functional and focuses on developing literacy, communication and numeracy skills as well as on independent living, social, vocational and self-advocacy skills, to the exclusion of, for example, creative activities (Griffiths 1994; Griffiths and Tennyson 1997). The balance and relevance of each of these components is contentious, particularly in relation to young people with severe or profound learning difficulties. For example the possibility of employment for some young people has been questioned. Other critics have challenged the importance of 'independence' or basic skills. More than 15 years ago Corbett observed, 'a narrow focus on basic skills impedes the quality of life and inhibits self-expression' (1989: 159) echoing a debate that persists today.

Some curriculum approaches emphasize the agency of young people reflected in the growing interest in personalized learning and choice. Young people are seen as consumers of services, shopping around for the programmes that best meet their aspirations and needs, shaping their identities through the choices they make. However Hughes et al. (2005) argue that young disabled people are excluded from these processes by the barriers and prejudices that remain within society. They suggest that the concept of real choice (and in this context what to learn, how to learn, when to learn and why) that accompanies notions of personalized learning is one that remains closed to many people with learning difficulties or disabilities. Barriers include practical difficulties such as transport arrangements, access to leisure and other community facilities and communication and attitudinal barriers. They also include temporal barriers, i.e., the failure of society to recognize that some people require longer to achieve certain tasks whether that be crossing the road or achieving a particular qualification. To this I would add emotional or affective barriers, since the concept of choice also implies changes in people's lives. Changes to routines or relationships built up over many years can appear threatening to the person themselves and to others in their lives, as we saw in Malcolm's father's response to his wish to leave school and travel independently.

A fundamental plank of the consumerist model is the notion of self-determination defined by Field et al. (1998: 2) as

> a combination of skills, knowledge and beliefs that enable a person to engage in goal-directed, self-regulated, autonomous behaviour. An understanding of one's strengths and limitations together with a belief in oneself as capable and effective are essential to self-determination. When acting on the basis of these skills and attitudes, individuals have greater ability to take control of their lives and assume the role of successful adults in our society.

However the concept of self-determination has also been criticized for emphasizing individual choice and control at the expense of community. Browder et al. (2001) argue for a concept of self-determination that is sensitive to cultural differences and that recognizes the importance of cultural and family ties. Maudslay et al.'s study of young Asian adults with learning difficulties concluded that notions of independence and self-determination have arisen out of a highly individualistic society where autonomy and individual choice are seen as ultimate goals (2003: 24). They argue that how young people wish to exercise their choice and control is likely to vary considerably between cultures.

In recent national curriculum guidance there has been a shift away from the learner as consumer to citizen. For instance the Tomlinson Report's recommendations on the 14–19 curriculum emphasized the need for young people to be effective as individuals and as members of their immediate social circles and wider society (DfES 2004b). The notion of personalized learning has also been modified. Leadbetter (2004) cites the best practice in special education and urges us to look beyond the consumerist model to one in which the individual becomes connected to the collective, so that they are shaping and regenerating their own communities. This means enabling learners to express their aspirations, needs and preferences; providing greater choice and a 'vocabulary of experiences' on which they can base their choices; assembling solutions around the learner not around the service providers; developing closer partnerships between, for instance, schools, colleges and work-based learning providers; providing advocacy where necessary; ensuring that funding follows individuals not services. This he believes will lead to individuals becoming more committed to and responsible for the quality of services and community life. At the group level similar processes may be used to regenerate communities through consulting on the changes that different groups would like to see in their communities and then giving them the tools to do so, e.g., young single mothers living on council estates; disaffected young men living in urban areas; elderly people living in rural communities.

Tisdall (1994) and Armstrong (2003) have both argued for models of provision for those with learning difficulties that reflect a belief and commitment to citizenship. Tisdall noted, 'Respecting the young person's human dignity – their worth as a person, their individuality, their ownership of their lives – should be the guiding principle of service provision' (1994: 12). The QCA's (2001) curriculum guidance for pupils with learning difficulties on personal, social and health education and citizenship also emphasizes both self-efficacy and community, listing, for example, the need for young people to:

- Move from contact with others in class and school to community
- Develop greater control and choice
- Adapt to change
- Move from the personal to a wider perspective
- Move from an immediate time perspective to thinking about the future

(QCA 2001: 4).

This final aim reflects the time-relatedness of transition. The curriculum recognizes that young people are exploring who they are and who they want to become in different settings and contexts, and that their ideas may change over time. Based on the earlier DOTS curriculum (decision making, opportunities, transitions, self-awareness) the DfES (2003b) defines the aims of career education and guidance as enabling *all* young people to:

- Understand themselves and the influences on them
- Investigate opportunities in learning and work
- Make and adjust plans to manage change and transition

Malian and Nevin (2002) also argue for a more dynamic and time-related understanding of the development of self-determination. They reviewed the evaluations of several programmes designed to improve the self-determination skills of young people with a range of special educational needs. While concluding that young people can acquire these skills they suggest that self-determination must be seen as fluid, developing across the life span and as strongly influenced by the contexts in which the young person finds themselves.

The following proposals draw a number of these ideas together and are summarized in Figure 7.1. The diagram illustrates the relationship between the curriculum, individualized planning procedures, the Connexions Service and other services that support the young people and their families/carers throughout the process. The curriculum is informed by and contributes to the individualized planning processes and procedures. However good transition procedures appear to be, unless young people are supported in their everyday experiences through the curriculum any plans are unlikely to become a reality. Effective interagency working can both open up new opportunities for young people and support their access to the curriculum through, for example, supporting their physical access or providing psychological or practical support. The Connexions Service advisers can contribute directly to the formal curriculum provided that opportunities are built into the

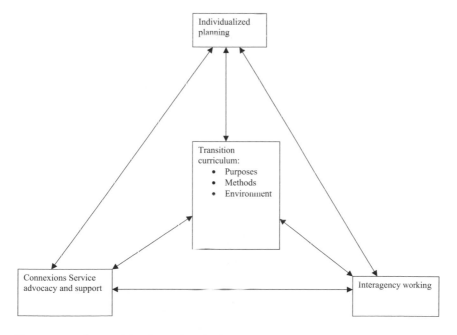

Figure 7.1 The transition-focused curriculum

programme to enable them to do so. But the services must also liaise closely with one another to support the individual planning process to ensure coherence and continuity. These proposals span both the period before and after leaving school, recognizing that for many young people this particular phase of their lives extends well into their 20s.

7.2 Curriculum

If it is to become more than just a bureaucratic exercise, planning for transition needs to be supported through and by the curriculum. The aspirations and educational needs of the young person should inform the curriculum and the curriculum should support the process of transition. In other words, education needs to become more 'transition-focused' (Kohler and Field 2003: 176). So programmes need to recognize and support the inherent messiness and unpredictability of the transition process as well as the fundamental educational needs of every young person during their transition from school and college. In this section I explore what some of those generic elements might be.

As I said at the outset of this book, the transition to adulthood for young people with learning difficulties and/or disabilities is both the same and different to how it is for all young people. So the fundamental purposes of the curriculum will be the same for everyone. Differences will occur in the degree and nature of the support and intervention that some learners with learning difficulties and disabilities require in developing and realizing their individual transition plans and in accessing the curriculum.

Three aspects of the transition-focused curriculum are discussed:

- Purposes
- Teaching approaches
- The learning environment

Purposes[1]

Exploring who I am and who I want to become
The transition-focused curriculum should enable young people to explore who they are, who they want to become and what they want to do. Exploring who we want to become starts from an early age but unlike other children, and for all sorts of reasons, those who are disabled or experience learning difficulties are rarely asked what they want to be when they grow up. Yet the opportunity to dream and fantasize is part of working out who we are and who we could become. Responding to these dreams and aspirations means actively listening to and engaging with what young people are saying. To say

that some people's opinions and ideas may be unrealistic is to miss the point. Many of us have unrealistic ambitions. The challenge is to recognize that dreams and aspirations are an essential part of exploring ideas and possibilities, and to work with the grain of those ideas in creative and flexible ways.

Experiencing new possibilities and opportunities

Providing new possibilities and opportunities is one means of helping young people explore who they are and who they want to become. Education can open up new and exciting possibilities that can stimulate new interests as well as enabling young people to experience and test out their ambitions over time. For example Maria's love of music was stimulated and developed by the college classes that she attended. Part of this process may then be to help learners rethink their ambitions and aspirations. Nasreen's introduction to law courts and the role of the barrister caused her to rethink her possible future career path. Young people can also reject possibilities on the basis of experience, as Stuart did after he had been on a college link course.

But providing opportunities is not enough. Learners require support in developing skills and capacities to take advantage of the opportunities available to them through, for example, being supported to reflect on their experiences and achievements and identifying what they need to learn or do next. The role of education is to help young people to develop these skills of reflection and planning.

A broad range of opportunities also enables people to develop what might be described as a 'vocabulary of experiences' on which to base future choices. It's easier to make decisions if you know what is involved and if you have experiences of expressing preferences and making choices in all areas of your life. Wehmeyer et al. (1998) argue that choice making, decision making and problem solving form a kind of overlapping hierarchy that, if incorporated into the lives of adults and young people with learning difficulties, can help them to: 'learn how to define the issue or problem about which a specific decision is to be made, collect information about their specific situation and use this information to identify options for consideration' (Wehmeyer et al. 1998: 14). Of course this argument presupposes a rational model of decision making, when in fact many decisions are made by default or as a result of compromise, as described in Chapter 3. Perhaps what is more important is developing within individuals the capacity to influence or take advantage of events which lead to the decision being made.

Activities such as work experience placements, visits, school/college link programmes or community-based projects can also provide opportunities for chance or serendipitous events to occur that can lead to a new interest, friendship or skill. New opportunities and encounters can trigger new interests and enthusiasms that may create important turning points in individuals' lives.

Using what you've got

Adolescent transitions are almost always characterized by flux as people move from familiar to new and unfamilar contexts and settings. Everyone remembers feelings of helplessness and 'not knowing anything' when moving to a new job or home but gradually we begin to adjust and make sense of our new sur-roundings. For some young people with learning difficulties or disabilities these initial periods of adjustment to, for instance, a new college or training programme may take longer and they rely on other people to recognize and build on the skills and strengths that they bring. Yet often what people can do gets lost or overlooked. In any learning situation it is important to recognize and capitalize on what the learner brings: their interests, motivations, skills and experiences as well as their personal aspirations. Advances in technology for transferring information, such as the use of memory sticks, means that young people can easily carry their progress files with them to provide evidence of their achievements. Professionals then have to decide, in collaboration with the learner and other interested parties, the most important skills and experi-ence for a learner to acquire in the time available. But what are they? In designing learning opportunities the locus of control needs to shift away from professionals towards the learners so that the learner can make choices and influence the nature of the curriculum offer, building on and using their existing skills to achieve their goals, as well as developing new skills.

Being proactive

Being listened to and having our personal views respected is an important aspect of developing a sense of self and control over our own destinies. This involves young people in deriving meaning from their experiences, refining their goals and aspirations, while discarding others, formulating a new plan and starting again.

This process also involves young people in making choices, although the rhetoric of choice belies its complexity as the casestudies in this book demonstrate. Supporting young people to make choices involves:

- developing an understanding of the concept of 'choice'
- communication skills
- having access to an advocate who can be relied on to communicate preferences as accurately as possible
- having a range of first-hand experiences to draw on
- good quality accessible information
- adequate time to reach decisions and make choices.

Involving self-advocacy groups or other role models or mentors in providing information about post-school and college opportunities helps to reinforce young people's view of themselves as agents of change in their own lives.

Adapting to change

Making choices generally leads to some form of change and during the transition years these changes can be far reaching. But changes in our lives can also be very threatening and upsetting. Learning to adapt to change involves people in learning how to learn, taking risks, problem solving and transferring their learning to new situations and activities. Yet aspects of special education provision can work in opposition to achieving these learning outcomes. Some special school staff for example may feel that colleges are unable to provide the level of support and consistency that learners require. Byers (1998), however, observes that the importance of support and consistency in working with learners with learning difficulties for instance can inhibit development and that, 'the balance between support and challenge, help and independence, protection and autonomy, and safe practice and risk taking in the social climate of the learning environment should be maintained under constant review' (p. 47). In other words, if learners are only exposed to that which is safe and predictable, they will never have the experience of taking risks and coping with the unpredictable, which in turn further disadvantages them in adapting to and coping with change in their adult lives. So the transition curriculum needs to provide carefully planned opportunities for young people to take risks and experience unexpected difficulties with decreasing levels of support and intervention. This delicate balance or tension between support and risk is summed up by the phrase 'independence without abandonment', which acknowledges 'both the autonomy and vulnerability of individuals' (Dee et al. 2003).

Maintaining and building friendships

Riddell et al. (2001) concluded that during periods of transition people with learning difficulties were more likely to lose friendships and social ties, while other studies have shown how far this aspect of young people's lives is neglected when planning for the transition from school (Raphael 2003). In this study a number of young people were influenced in their choice of college as a result of the difficulties they had experienced in making friends during link programmes at their local secondary schools. Friendships often develop through shared interests and activities and for friendships to flourish it may be necessary to plan some kind of systematic intervention. Creating new and inclusive leisure, cultural, sport and social opportunities may become easier through the extended schools scheme and the Disability Equality Scheme. Existing examples of work in this area include:

- Peer support programmes linking disabled and non-disabled young people with similar interests in mainstream schools or colleges of further education (Hayhoe 1998, 1999);

- Circles of Friends that build on and foster networks of social support in community settings (Wertheimer 1995; Jay 2003);
- Developing links with local authority leisure facilities and projects (DfES 2004d).

Teaching approaches to support transition

Throughout this book various suggestions have been made as to how to facilitate learners' involvement in the transition process. Many individual education or learning plans emphasize what is to be taught (content) but they also need to describe what kind of strategies are likely to be successful with particular learners. The choice of methods should also be influenced by what is being taught. Emphasis will need to be given to methods that

- Build on previous learning and raise attainment through target-setting; breaking down tasks into small steps; measuring success against pre-specified outcomes; developing specific skills such as communication or literacy skills that provide access to learning across the curriculum.
- Support young people to participate in the learning process so that the learner and the teacher are both learners. Students are involved in reflecting on and reviewing their own progress, setting new targets and expressing learning preferences and choices.
- Involve young people in taking risks, problem solving and learning how to learn. As well as learning specific strategies, students require opportunities to learn from experience and solve problems for themselves, gradually reducing the levels of support and intervention that are provided.
- Recognize that learning takes place in different contexts and settings in which the individual may assume different roles, have different experiences and may be subject to different expectations. The relationships between the different settings can also influence learning, e.g., the relationship between the home and school; college and self-advocacy group; college and workplace.

The learning environment

Like all young people, those with learning difficulties and/or disabilities will experience a range of different settings both in their everyday lives and as they leave school and move into further or higher education and training. Different environments present different opportunities for learning. These different environments are sometimes described as formal, non-formal and informal education (OECD 2004):

- Formal learning takes place in organized, structured settings such as schools, colleges, universities or work-based training. For most people this leads to some kind of certification;
- Non-formal learning refers to organized activities with a learning component, e.g., youth and community activities;
- Informal learning occurs by chance or during everyday activities and encounters, e.g., watching television, reading the paper or having a conversation.

Increasingly, however, the boundaries between these different types of learning opportunities are seen as blurred and permeable (Colley et al. 2003). Formal learning at school or college can open up opportunities for informal or non-formal learning, while youth and community activities, for instance, may include some form of accreditation. Elements of non-formal activities can become formalized, e.g., developing the skills required to participate in a self-advocacy group or practicing home management skills can become part of the formally structured curriculum. Non-formal activities, such as theatre groups or art projects which spread over a sustained period of time, can create rich and valuable opportunities for developing a range of important skills for life. Finally, informal opportunities for learning can occur in formal and informal settings, e.g., how to use a new mobile phone or how to deal with a problem.

Access to learning opportunities
Young people with learning difficulties and/or disabilities require access to the full range of learning opportunities implied by this typology. Important skills include communication, the wider key skills (problem solving, improving own learning and performance and working with others) and travel training. Access becomes easier where there are close relationships between formal and informal learning so that one supports and builds on the other. Research by Holmes and Fillary (2000) shows how people with learning difficulties often lack the skills to engage in casual exchanges in the workplace, essential to building relationships. Role plays and other communication exercises can offer learners greater confidence in these casual exchanges. Access will also require additional resources and interagency collaboration to support participation in community-based activities, for example, at the local leisure centre or church. This may mean gaining support from a mentor, citizen advocate or other community resource.

Potential of the learning context

This typology also challenges providers to consider the importance of the context of learning and its influence on the nature of that learning. Special schools may well feel that 'we can do what they do at college better here'. However, opportunities for learning are created through and by the learning environment so the more diverse the environment and opportunities for social interaction, the richer the potential for learning. For example, Maria joined a music class at her local further education college one day a week. At first she was unable to tolerate the noise and bustle of the refectory, so her learning support assistant took her a drink and snack to the classroom. Then, gradually over the course of three months, Maria's support assistant helped her to develop her tolerance of the refectory so that eventually she was able to take her break alongside everyone else. In this instance Maria's support assistant was able to exploit the environment and the naturally occurring events to boost Maria's confidence and encourage greater autonomy and independence. It is important to look beyond the confines of the formal learning environment, i.e., the classroom or workshop to exploit what the community and other social settings have to offer, including the chance to widen the network of people with whom the learner has contact.

7.3   Individual planning and personalized learning

The *Code of Practice* requires that every young person with a statement of special educational needs has an individual transition plan from Year 9 onwards that is reviewed annually until such time as they leave school. Those without statements but who have been identified as having special educational needs can also benefit from a systematic and regular review of their aspirations and support needs. Although colleges and work-based training providers are not required to maintain transition plans, these plans should be kept under review since most young people will continue to require substantial support, whether the next step is into further education, training or employment.

Central to the transition planning process are the young person and their parents/carers. The *Code of Practice* emphasizes the centrality of their involvement in transition planning but, as discussed in Chapter 3, tensions and dilemmas may result from their different perspectives and priorities. As the young person grows older the role of parents and carers becomes less clear – many wish to be and indeed have no choice but to continue to be closely involved in supporting their son or daughter, but post-school providers often regard parents as interfering in what they see as the young person's growing autonomy. As Smart (2004) notes, 'Staff in adult placements have been reported to place autonomy above partnership with parents' (p. 129). In this case the role of the Connexions personal adviser or their equivalent becomes vital to maintaining or building bridges between all concerned.

The young person's aspirations and their support needs as well as those of their family's are recorded on the transition plan and then regularly reviewed. The learner's aspirations and their needs will have different implications for different services. For education the transition plan should inform the student's learning plan, sometimes referred to as individual learning plans or individual education plans. For example, Malcolm recognized that to become a van driver's mate he needed to read signs and maps and Gavin's wish to work with animals could have been supported through a work experience placement.

In practice, different services are expected to carry out separate assessments of individuals and develop related action plans. But it is often difficult for young people and their parents to see how these relate to each other. To some extent these different approaches to planning are now jostling for position. For example, Connexions are required to carry out a holistic assessment called an APIR (assessment, planning, implementation and review). The extent to which this process is accessible to all learners varies. In addition all young people with learning difficulties leaving school and who are eligible for support from social services must have a person-centred plan. Person-centred planning approaches are based on the premise that the outcome of the process is the life that the person wants, not the plan itself. Some schools have begun using person-centred planning to replace transition plans, since they fulfill many similar purposes. Transition planning would undoubtedly benefit from using more interactive approaches than at present but it is important to remember that not all young people with special educational needs will fall under the remit of social services and require a person-centred plan. The driving force behind any rationalization of these multiple processes and procedures must be to the advantage of young people and not as a means of holding professionals accountable to central regulators.

7.4 Interagency support

The two final sections in this chapter discuss the role of support services including Connexions in supporting the transition process. As well as the Connexions Service the range of statutory services involved could include for instance social services, housing, health, youth justice and leisure services, as well as community groups such as self-advocacy groups and other voluntary organizations.

The experiences of the young people and their families recounted in this book are illustrative of the kind of difficulties experienced by many others such as feeling alienated by the language that is used, the paucity of information and access to post-school health care determined by geography rather than need. The difficulties and problems in interagency working have been widely documented, not just in relation to the transition phase but across the life span of people with disabilities (Lacey and Lomas 1993; Morris 1999; McIntosh and Whittaker 2000; Lacey 2001; Riddell and Tett 2001; Byers et al. 2002). Many problems commonly associated with interagency working are exacerbated during the school-leaving phase including:

- Discontinuity between child and adult services
- Differences in eligibility criteria for services such as access to transport, personal assistance, benefits
- The large number of services that are involved
- Multiple assessments that do not relate to each other and that are not used to inform planning
- Poor communication between service providers, including failure to share information
- Disputes over funding
- Lack of clarity and/or understanding of each other's roles and responsibilities
- Different priorities
- Access to health services such as physiotherapy, speech and language support, psychiatry determined by geography rather then need
- Fragile networks that rely on relationships between individuals rather than on robust strategic and operational frameworks
- Rapid staff turnover.

In Chapter 2, I outlined the changing legislative framework describing how government policy is seeking to develop 'wrap around' or 'joined up' services placing children and young people aged 0–19 and their families at the centre of service provision. These fundamental and long overdue reforms have significant implications for the management and support of transitions, although the extent to which authorities will see this area of work as a priority remains to be seen.

Ideally these changes provide an opportunity to create strong and continuous pathways of support, to mirror the proposals on the 14–19 curriculum. The current separation between child and adult services and between schools and colleges has led to young people falling between the administrative cracks. The Local Safeguarding Children's Boards on which a wide range of agencies are represented including schools, health services, social services, police and the local Learning and Skills Councils must produce a Children and Young People's Plan. This strategic level plan should be informed by learners' individual transition plans or person-centred plans. Systems are required to enable the information contained in individual plans to be summarized and then aggregated across the authority to allow areas for development to emerge such as gaps in existing provision or staff training priorities to emerge.

Second, Children's Trusts as well as the proposals in the green paper, *Youth Matters*, should make it easier for services to respond more holistically to the dreams and aspirations as well as the needs of young people, looking beyond their traditional boundaries. Young people's aspirations touch all aspects of their future lives – social life, career, life style, living arrangements, education, marriage, interests, friendships, travel and politics. Their needs in realizing these dreams are often interdependent and merge one with another. For example, to start work Malcolm needed to be able to travel independently, but before he could do that his father needed to overcome his fears; and Kim wanted to join the local youth club but her mother needed help with her own anxieties before she would allow Kim to do so. The kind of support required by Kim, Malcolm and their families demanded close liaison and collaboration between a number of different services: education, family therapy, social services and the youth service. The Children's Trusts are developing new protocols governing how the services work together, assessment procedures and ways of sharing information. Perhaps more importantly some are beginning to pool their budgets (UEA/NCB 2004).

There is a good deal riding on these initiatives but the success factors are likely to remain the same. At strategic and operational levels these are the need for:

- Clear leadership
- Common vision
- Good communication systems
- Joint training
- Stable resources that are pooled
- Protocols governing how services will work together
- Trust
- Time.

What the young person requires is:

- A key worker or named person
- Continuity of personnel
- Clear information
- Someone to speak up on their behalf when necessary
- To be listened to and taken seriously.

The person who can fulfill these requirements for many young people with special educational needs has become the Connexions Service personal adviser. The proposed changes described here have considerable consequences for the future of the Connexions Service.

7.5 The Connexions Service and its future

In Figure 7.1, Connexions are seen as the link between the individual, their aspirations and needs, their family, education and the support services, acting as advocate and broker. As discussed in Chapter 2, where Connexions personal advisers work effectively they have made a significant difference to the experience of leaving school for many young people. They offer the kind of objective advice and support that Mr Simpson said that he wanted for himself and James. Personal advisers contribute to the curriculum through working directly with young people on a one to one or small group basis as well as through providing ideas and resources for careers education and guidance programmes. To work successfully they need to understand how the young person communicates and how to build trusting relationships.

Of course some of the young people who Connexions work with are not in education, employment or training (NEETs) and will have followed similar routes to Kylie, Gavin and Malcolm. These young people are often difficult to contact once they have dropped out of the system, they are known to a variety of services such as youth offending teams, social services, drug support teams and are often mistrustful of officialdom. Personal advisers need to be proactive in reaching out to them and invest time and commitment in establishing a trusting relationship.

The extent to which the Connexions Service has achieved a totally person-centred service is open to question as organizational and logistical considerations continue to determine their patterns of work. If a young person attends a mainstream school they are more likely to be supported by a generic adviser whereas those in special schools are more likely to be supported by a specialist adviser. In other services these distinctions have been merged but with advisers retaining their individual specialisms. So the school that a young person attends may determine not only their post-school destination but the nature of any support they receive. Second, some services have found it difficult to organize continuity of support between school and college. Consequently the adviser who supports them at school is unlikely to be the same person who supports them at college.

To what extent will the new service arrangements affect the way in which Connexions Services work? Coles et al. (2004) are optimistic that the inter-agency framework which includes Connexions in the single tier local authority partnerships will improve the quality of local provision through bringing them closer to tried and trusted partnerships that are more representative of local needs than existing regional management structures.

Rowland-Cosby et al. (2004) on the other hand are more cautious believing that the devolution of Connexions Service budgets to local authorities could compromise the independence of the service. They also believe, however, that the personal advisers constitute a ready made group of professionals able to take over the role of key or lead worker in multi-agency teams.

7.6 Conclusions

In this final chapter I have summarized what I believe to be the essential ingredients in improving the transition to adulthood for young people with special educational needs. I have argued that the experience of making decisions and leaving school are fundamentally the same for all young people and thus the underlying purposes of the transition curriculum should also be the same. As we go through life events may occur that throw us off course and young people with special educational needs and their families are no exception to this. Some have the resources to cope while others may not. The task of the services is to provide support that moulds itself around the young person and their families, that is sensitive to their changing needs while enabling them to move towards the goals and aspirations that they have for their future lives.

Note

1   A version of this section also appears in Dee et al. (in press) Learning for Living: Person Centred Approaches and adults with learning difficulties. Leicester: NIACE/DfES.

Improving transition planning

1   As a staff team review the aims and purposes of the curriculum in your school or college. What are the underlying aims and purposes of what you do? Compare these to the six curriculum purposes that are outlined in this chapter.

2   Working as an interdisciplinary team, identify ways in which you can work together to support the curriculum beyond the formal setting of the school or college. What use do you make of community-based activities or programmes?

3   What steps do you take to support students in reflecting on their feelings and experiences as a young disabled adult? Are opportunities included in tutorial sessions or careers education and guidance programmes?

4 How are adults with disabilities, including members of local self-advocacy groups, involved in working with young people?

5 Find out whether your local authority has an interagency protocol that governs 14–25 provision for young people with learning difficulties and/or disabilities. What are the implications for:

- How you work with learners?
- How your organization works?
- How you work with parents?
- How you work together with professionals from other services?

Appendix: Profiles of casestudy pupils and their families

Project name	Age at first contact	Gender	Disability	Education path	Aspirations	Mother's job	Father's job	Ethnicity
Andrew Bailey	14	M	Profoundly deaf	Residential special school for deaf, located in mainstream 2ndry school. Specialist college for deaf and mainstream college	Electrician or film star	Unknown	Electrician	White
Costas Demetrios	15	M	Moderate learning difficulties	Day special school and then FE unit in same school	To have a girlfriend	Hairdresser	Post Office transport manager	Greek-Cypriot

Project name	Age at first contact	Gender	Disability	Education path	Aspirations	Mother's job	Father's job	Ethnicity
David Francis	13	M	Profoundly deaf	Day special school for deaf. Residential specialist college for deaf and mainstream college	To become an actor. Look after animals.	BSL Communicator	Construction worker and university student	White
Gavin Stone	14	M	Emotional and behavioural difficulties	Comprehensive school: excluded. 2ndry comprehensive school: truanted	Zookeeper. Get married, have two children, a dog and a snake.	Foster mother: Prison officer Birth mother: Unknown	Foster father: Unknown Birth father: Unknown	Black Afro-Caribbean
James Simpson	15	M	Physical disabilities	Residential special school. Residential specialist college	A policeman but later office work. Live independently in a flat.	Nursery nurse	Plumber and then made redundant	White
Kim Doyle	16	F	Moderate learning difficulties	Day special school and then FE unit in the same school	Computer work in a bank. Go to local youth club.	Classroom assistant	Supermarket store man	White

Project name	Age at first contact	Gender	Disability	Education path	Aspirations	Mother's job	Father's job	Ethnicity
Kylie Long	13	F	Moderate learning difficulties	Various comprehensive schools and then dropped out. Work experience in nursery and then dropped out.	Unsure – computing; nursery nurse; work with animals.	Various – shop assistant; barmaid	Unknown	White
Malcolm Lewis	15	M	Moderate learning difficulties	Day special school and then FE unit in same school. Dropped out in Year 12	Van driver's mate. Live in house in Enfield with cat and dog.	Full-time housewife	Unemployed	White
Maria Constandis	18	F	Profound and complex learning difficulties	Day special school and residential care	Unknown	FE lecturer	Unknown	Greek-Cypriot
Nasreen Hussein	15	F	Blind	Day special school. Residential specialist college.	Psychologist or barrister	Full-time housewife	Self-employed	Pakistani
Sandra Harding	15	F	Physical disabilities and learning difficulties	Day special school. P/T mainstream college.	Not to leave home	Personnel assistant	Unemployed	White

Project name	Age at first contact	Gender	Disability	Education path	Aspirations	Mother's job	Father's job	Ethnicity
Stuart Brown	13	M	Emotional and behavioural difficulties and learning difficulties	Comprehensive school	Carpenter	School dinner lady	Lorry driver	White

References

ALI (Adult Learning Inspectorate) (2004) *Chief Inspectors Annual Report*. http//: www.ALI.gov.uk

Allan, J. (1999) *Actively Seeking Inclusion: Pupils with Special Needs in Mainstream Schools*. London: Falmer Press.

Anderson, E.M. and Clarke, L. (1982) *Disability in Adolescents*. London: Methuen.

Armstrong, D. (1995) *Power and Partnership in Education: Parents, Children and Special Educational Needs*. London: Routledge.

Armstrong, D. (2003) *Experiences of Special Education: Re-evaluating policy and practice through life stories*. London: RoutledgeFalmer.

Armstrong, D. and Davies, P. (1995) The transition from school to adulthood: aspiration and careers advice for young adults with learning and adjustment difficulties, *British Journal of Special Education*, 22(2): 70–5.

Avis, D. (1985) Deinstitutionalisation jet lag, in H. Turnbull and A. Turnbull (eds) *Parents Speak out. Then and Now*. Columbus: Charles Merrill.

Ball, S.J. (1994) *Education Reform*. Buckingham: Open University Press.

Ball, S.J., Maguire, M. and Macrae, S. (2000) *Choices, Pathways and Transitions Post 16: New Youth, New Economies in the Global City*. London: RoutledgeFalmer.

Baron, J. (1988) *Thinking and Deciding*. Cambridge: Cambridge University Press.

Beckman, P. (ed.) (1996) *Strategies for Working with Families of Young Children with Disabilities*. London: Paul H. Brookes.

Bell, D.E., Raiffa, H. and Tversky, A. (1988) Descriptive, normative and prescriptive interactions in decision making, in D. E. Bell, H. Raiffa and A. Tversky (eds) *Decision-making: Descriptive, Normative and Prescriptive Interactions*. Cambridge: Cambridge University Press.

Brannen, J. (1996) Discourses of adolescence: young people's independence and autonomy within families, in J. Brannen and M. O'Brien, *Children in Families: Research and Policy*. London: Falmer Press.

Bronfenbrenner, U. (1979) *The Ecology of Human Development*. London: Harvard University Press.

Bronfenbrenner, U. and Morris, P. (1998) *Handbook of Child Psychology*. London: Wiley.

Browder, D.M., Wood, W.M., Test, D.W., Karvonen, M. and Algozzine, B. (2001) Reviewing resources on self determination: a map for teachers, *Remedial and Special Education*, 22(4): 233–55.

Byers, R. (1998) Personal and social development for pupils with learning difficulties, in C. Tilstone, L. Florian and R. Rose (eds) *Promoting Inclusive Practice*. London: Routledge.

Byers, R., Dee, L., Hayhoe, H. and Maudslay, L. (2002) *Enhancing Quality of Life: Facilitating Transitions for People with Profound and Complex Learning Difficulties*. London: Skill/University of Cambridge.

Cabinet Office (2005) *Improving the Life Chances of Disabled People*. http://www.strategy.gov.uk/downloads/work_areas/disability_report

Carnaby, S., Lewis, P., Martin, D., Naylor, J. and Stewart, D. (2003) Participation in transition review meetings: a case study of young people with learning disabilities leaving a special school, *British Journal of Special Education*, 30(4): 187–93.

Carpenter, B. (1997) *Families in Context*. London: David Fulton.

CERI (Centre for Educational Research and Innovation) (1986) *Young People with Handicaps: The Road to Adulthood*. Paris: Organisation for Economic Co-operation and Development.

CERI (Centre for Educational Research and Innovation) (1994) *Disabled Youth and Employment*. Paris: Organisation for Economic Co-operation and Development.

Christenson, S.L. and Sheridan, S.M. (2001) *Schools and Families: Creating Connections for Essential Learning*. London: The Guildford Press.

Clarke, A. and Hirst, M. (1989) Disability in Adulthood: Ten-year Follow-up of Young People with Disabilities, *Disability, Handicap and Society*, 4(3): 271–83.

Coles, B., Britton, L. and Hicks, L. (2004) *Building Better Connections: Inter-agency Work and the Connexions Service*. Bristol: Policy Press.

Colley, H., Hodkinson, P. and Malcolm, J. (2003) *Informality and Formality in Learning: A Report for the Learning and Skills Research Centre*. London: LSDA.

Cooley, W.C. and Moeschler, J.B. (1993) Counselling in the health care relationship, in G.H. Powers and L.E. Singer (eds) *Families, Disability and Empowerment*. London: Paul H. Brookes.

Corbett, J. (1989) The quality of life in the independence curriculum, *Disability, Handicap and Society*, 4(2): 145–63.

Crow, L. (2003) Including all of our lives: renewing the social model of disability, in M. Nind, J. Rix, K. Sheehy and K. Simmons (eds) *Inclusive Education: Diverse Perspectives*. London: David Fulton.

Dee, L., Florian, L., Porter, J. and Robertson, C. (2003) Developing curriculum guidance for person-centred transitions, in D. Rodrigues (ed.) *Perspectivas sobre a Inclusao: da Educacao a Sociedade* (Perspectives on Inclusion: From Education to Society). Porto: Porto Editoria.

Department for Trade and Industry (1993) *Trade Union Reform and Employment Rights Act*. London: HMSO.

Dewson. S., Aston, J., Bates, P., Ritchie, H. and Dyson, A. (2004) *Post 16 Transitions: A Longitudinal Study of Young People with Special Educational Need. Wave Two*. Nottingham: DfES.

DES (Department of Education and Science) (1988) *Education Reform Act*. London: HMSO.

DfE (Department for Education) (1992) *Further and Higher Education (FHE) Act.* London: HMSO.

DfE (Department for Education) (1993) *Education Act.* London: HMSO.

DfE (Department for Education) (1994) *Code of Practice on the Identification and Assessment of Special Educational Needs.* London: HMSO.

DfEE (Department for Education and Employment) (2000a) *The Learning and Skills Act.* London: HMSO.

DfEE (Department for Education and Employment) (2000b) *Connexions: The Best Start in Life for Every Young Person.* London: DfEE.

DfES (Department for Education and Skills) (2001) *Special Educational Needs Code of Practice: Draft Code of Practice laid before Parliament under section 314 (3) of the Education Act on 20th June 2001.* http://www.dfes.gov.uk/index.htm

DfES (Department for Education and Skills) (2003a) *Every Child Matters.* Nottingham: DfES.

DfES (Department for Education and Skills) (2003b) *Careers Education and Guidance: National Framework.* http://www.dfes.gov.uk

DfES (Department for Education and Skills) (2004a) *Removing Barriers to Achievement.* Nottingham: DfES.

DfES (Department for Education and Skills) (2004b) *14–19 Curriculum and Qualifications Reform: Final Report of the Working Group on 14–19 Reform.* Nottingham: DfES.

DfES (Department for Education and Skills) (2004c) *The Children Act.* Norwich: HMSO.

DfES (Department for Education and Skills) (2004d) *Youth Matters.* Nottingham: DfES.

DfES (Department for Education and Skills) (2005) *14–19 Education and Skills White Paper.* Nottingham: DfES.

DoH (Department of Health) (1989) *Children's Act.* London: HMSO.

DoH (Department of Health) (1990) *National Health Service and Community Care Act.* London: HMSO.

DoH (Department of Health) (2001a) *Children (Leaving Care) Act.* Norwich: HMSO.

DoH (Department of Health) (2001b) *Valuing People: A New Strategy for Learning Disability for the 21st Century.* Norwich: HMSO.

DoH (Department of Health) (2004) *The National Service Framework.* http://dh.gov.uk/PolicyandGuidance/HealthandSocialCareTopics/ChildrensServices

Dyson, A., Meagher, N. and Robson, E. (2002) Where have they gone? Issues in transition and progression for special school leavers, *Journal of Research in Special Educational Needs*, 2(2), June. www.nasen.uk.com/ejournal

European Agency for Development in Special Needs Education (2002) *Transition from School to Employment.* Middlefart: Brussels.

FEFC (Further Education Funding Council) (1996) *Inclusive Learning: Report of the Learning Difficulties and/or Disabilities Committee.* London: HMSO.

Field, S., Martin, J., Miller, R., Ward, M. and Wehmeyer, M. (1998) *A Practical Guide to Teaching Self Determination*. Reston CA: Council for Exceptional Children.

Florian, L., Dee, L., Byers, R. and Maudslay, L. (2000) What happens after the age of 14? Mapping transitions for pupils with profound and complex learning difficulties, *British Journal of Special Education*, 16(1): 124–8.

Foskett, N.H. and Hesketh, A.J. (1997) Constructing choice in contiguous and parallel markets: institutional and school leavers responses to the new post-16 market place, *Oxford Review of Education*, 23(3): 299–319.

Gambetta, D. (1987) *Were They Pushed or Did They Jump?* Cambridge: Cambridge University Press.

Gascoigne, E. (1995) *Working with Parents as Partners in Special Educational Needs*. London: Fulton.

Gottfredson, L.S. (1981) Circumspection and Compromise: A Developmental Theory of Occupational Aspirations, *Journal of Counselling Psychology*, 28(6): 545–79.

Greenfield, P., Keller, H. Fuligni, A. and Maynard, A. (2003) Cultural Pathways through Universal Development, *Annual Review of Psychology*, 54: 461–90.

Griffiths, M. (1994) *Transition to Adulthood*. London: Fulton.

Griffiths, M. and Tennyson, C. (1997) *The Extended Curriculum: Meeting the Needs of Young People*. London: David Fulton.

Grove, B. and Giraud-Saunders, A. (2003) Connecting with Connexions: the role of the personal adviser with young people with special educational and support needs, *Support for Learning*, February, 18(1): 12–17.

Harry, B. (1992) *Cultural Diversity, Families, and the Special Education System*. London: Teachers College Press.

Hayhoe, H. (1998) Peer integration in a further education college: evaluating the outcomes for mainstream students and their peers with severe learning difficulties. Unpublished PhD thesis, University of London Institute of Education.

Hayhoe, H. (1999) What happens when students with severe learning difficulties interact in an inclusive college? *Skill Journal Research Supplement*, April, 63: 1–13.

Heifetz, L. (1980) From consumer to middleman: emerging roles for parents in the network of services for retarded children, in R. Abidin (ed.) *Parent Education and Intervention Handbook*. Springfield, IL: Charles C. Thomas.

Heslop, P., Mallett, R., Simons, K. and Ward, L. (2002) *Bridging the Divide at Transition: What Happens for Young People with Learning Difficulties and their Families?* Kidderminster: British Institute of Learning Disabilities.

HMSO (1996) *Disability Discrimination Act*. Norwich: HMSO.

HMSO (2001) Special Educational Needs and Disability Discrimination Act. Norwich: HMSO.

Hodkinson, P. (1995) Careers and markets: structure and agency in the transition to work. PhD thesis, University of Exeter.

Hodkinson, P. and Sparkes, A.C. (1997) Careership: a sociological theory of career decision making, *British Journal of Sociology of Education*, 18(1): 29–43.

Hodkinson, P., Sparkes, A.C. and Hodkinson, H. (1996) *Triumphs and Tears: Young People, Markets and the Transition from School to Work*. London: David Fulton.

Holmes, J. and Fillary, R. (2000) Handling small talk at work: challenges for workers with intellectual disabilities, *International Journal of Disability, Development and Education*, 47(3): 273–91.

Hornby, G. and Kidd, R. (2001) Transfer from special to mainstream: ten years later, *British Journal of Special Education*, March, 28(1): 10–17.

Hughes, B., Russell, R. and Patterson, K. (2005) Nothing to be had off the peg: consumption, identity and the immobolization of young disabled people, *Disability and Society*, January, 20(1): 3–17.

Jay, N. (2003) The Circles Network CREDO Project, *Support for Learning*, 18(1): 24–8.

Jenkinson, J. (1993) Who shall decide? The relevance of theory and research to decision-making by people with an intellectual disability, *Disability, Handicap and Society*, 8(4): 361–75.

Kelsoe, T., French, D. and Fernandez, M. (2005) Stress and coping in primary caregivers of children with a disability: a qualitative approach using the Lazarus and Folkman Process Model of Coping, *Journal of Research in Special Education*, November, 5(1): 3–10.

Kohler, P. and Field, S. (2003) Transition-focused education: foundation for the future, *The Journal of Special Education*, 37(3): 174–83.

Kvaslund, R. (2004) Schools as environments for social learning–shaping mechanisms? Comparisons of smaller and larger rural schools in Norway, *Scandinavian Journal of Educational Research*, 48(4): 347–71.

Lacey, P. (2001) *Support Partnerships: Collaboration in Action*. London: David Fulton.

Lacey, P. and Lomas, J. (1993) *Support Services and the Curriculum: A Practical Guide to Collaboration*. London: David Fulton.

Laragy, C. (2004) Self-determination within Australian School transition programmes for students with a disability, *Disability and Society*, 19(5): 519–30.

Lazarus, R.S. (1993) From psychological stress to the emotions: a history of changing outlooks, *Annual Review of Psychology*, 44: 1–21.

Leadbetter, C. (2004) *Personalisation through Participation: A New Script for Public Services*. London: Demos.

Levinson, E.M. (1998) *Transition: Facilitating the Post-school Adjustment of Students with Disabilities*. Oxford: Westview Press.

Macadam, M. and Sutcliffe, J. (1996) *Still a Chance to Learn? A Report on the Impact of the Further and Higher Education Act on Education for Adults with Learning Difficulties*. Leicester: NIACE.

McGinty, J. and Fish, J. (1992) *Learning Support for Young People in Transition: Leaving School for Further Education and Work*. Buckingham: Open University Press.

McIntosh, B. and Whittaker, A. (eds) (2000) *Unlocking the Future: Developing New Life Styles with People who have Complex Disabilities*. London: King's Fund.

Malian, I. and Nevin, A. (2002) A Review of Self-Determination Literature, *Remedial and Special Education*, 23(2): 68–74.

Mansell, J. and Beadle-Brown, J. (2004) Person-centred planning or person-centred action? Policy and practice in intellectual disability services, *Journal of Applied Research in Intellectual Disabilities*, 17: 1–9.

Maudslay, L. (2003) Policy changes in post school learning for people with disabilities and learning difficulties and the implications for practice, *Support for Learning*, 18(1): 6–11.

Maudslay, L., Rafique, A. and Uddin, A. (2003) *Aasha: Working with Young People with a Learning Difficulty from a South Asian Background.* London: Skill National Bureau of Students with Disabilities.

Mellers, B.A., Schwartz, A. and Cooke, A.D.J. (1998) Judgement and Decision-making, *Annual Review of Psychology*, 49: 447–77.

Mental Health Foundation (2002) *Count Us In: The Report of the Committee of Enquiry into Meeting the Mental Health Needs of Young People with learning disabilities.* London: Foundation for People with learning disabilities/ Mental Health Foundation.

Merriam, S.B. (1999) Time as the integrative factor, in M.C. Clark and R.S. Caffarella (eds) *An Update on Adult Development Theory: New Ways of Thinking About the Life Course.* San Francisco: Josey-Bass Publishers.

Miner, C.A. and Bates, P.E. (1997) The effect of person centred planning activities on the IEP/transition planning process, *Education and Training in Mental Retardation and Developmental Disabilities*, June: 105–11.

Mitchell, W. (1999) Leaving special school: the next step and future aspirations, *Disability and Society*, 14(6): 753–70.

Morris, J. (1999) *Move on Up: Supporting Young Disabled People in their Transition to Adulthood.* Ilford: Barnardos.

Morrow, V. and Richards, M. (1996) *Transitions to Adulthood: A Family Matter.* York: Joseph Rowntree Foundation.

Norwich, B. (2000) *Education and Psychology in Interaction.* London: Routledge.

O'Bryan, A., Simons, K., Beyer, S. and Grove, B. (2000) *A Framework for Supported Employment.* York: Joseph Rowntree Foundation.

ODPM (Office of the Deputy Prime Minister) (2003) *Housing In England 2002/3.* London: The Stationery Office.

OECD (Organisation for Economic Co-operation and Development) (2004) *Education at a glance: Briefing Note United Kingdom.* http//:www.oecd.org

Ofsted (2004a) *Why Colleges Fail.* http//:www.ofsted.gov.uk

Osted (Office for Standards in Education) (2004b) *Annual Report of Her Majesty's Chief Inspector of Schools: Standards and Quality in Education 2002/03.* www.ofsted.gov.uk

Oyserman, D. and Markus, H.R. (1990) Possible selves and delinquency, *Journal of Personality and Social Psychology*, 59(1): 112–25.

Ozga, J. (2000) *Policy Research in Educational Settings: Contested Terrain*. Buckingham: Open University Press.

Pell, E.C. and Cohen, E.P. (1995) Parents and Advocacy Systems: A Family Systems Theory, in M. Reynolds, M. Wang and H. Walberg (eds) *Handbook of Special and Remedial Education*. Oxford: Pergamon.

Price, L. and Patton, J.R. (2003) A New World Order: Connecting Adult Development Theory to Learning Disabilities, *Remedial and Special Education*, 24(6): 328–38.

Putnam, R. and Goss, K. A. (2002) Introduction, in R. Putnam (ed.) *Democracies in Flux*. New York: Oxford University Press.

QCA (Qualifications and Curriculum Authority) (2001) *Planning, Teaching and Assessing the Curriculum for Pupils with Learning Difficulties: Personal, Social and Health Education and Citizenship*. London: QCA.

QCA (Qualifications and Curriculum Authority) (2004) *Play Your Part*. London: QCA.

Raphael, V. (2003) *Parents experiences of transition*, Unpublished paper presented at Eastern Region Valuing People Conference, Newmarket Racecourse Conference Center, 26 September.

Reay, D. (1996) Contextualising choice: social power and parental involvement, *British Educational Research Journal*, 22(5): 581–96.

Riddell, S. and Tett, L. (2001) Education, social justice and inter-agency working: joined-up or fractured policy? in S. Riddell and L. Tett (eds) *Education, Social Justice and Inter-agency Working*. London: Routledge.

Riddell, S., Baron, S. and Wilson, A. (2001) *The Learning Society and People with Learning Difficulties*. Bristol: The Policy Press.

Riddell, S., Brown, S. and Duffield, J. (1994) Conflicts of policies and models: the case of specific learning difficulties, in S. Brown and S. Riddell (eds) *Special Educational Needs in the Market Place*. London: Routledge.

Riddell, S., Ward, K. and Thomson, G. (1993) *Transition to Adulthood for Young People with Special Educational Needs*. Edinburgh: Moray House Publications.

Riddell, S., Wilson, A. and Baron, S. (1999) Captured customers: people with learning difficulties in the social market, *British Educational Research Journal*, 25(4): 445–61.

Roberts, K. (1971) *From School to Work: A Study of the Youth Employment*. Dawlish, Devon: W. J. Holman.

Routledge, M. and Gitsham, N. (2004) Putting person centred planning in its proper place? *Tizard Learning Disability Review*, 9(3): 21–6.

Rowland-Crosby, N., Giraud-Saunders, A. and Swift, P. (2004) *Developing Connexions*. http//:www.learning disabilities.org.uk

Rusteimer, S. (2000) Listening for inclusion in further education, Paper presented at the International Special Education Congress, University of Manchester, 24–8 July.

Sandow, S. (1994) *Whose Special Need?* London: Paul Chapman Publishers.

Smart, M (2004) Transition planning and the needs of young people and their carers: the alumni project, *British Journal of Special Education*, 13(3): 128–37.

Thomas, G. and Loxley, A. (2001) *Deconstructing Special Education and Constructing Inclusion*. Buckingham: Open University Press.

Tisdall, E.K.M. (1994) Why not consider citizenship? A critique of post school transitional models for young disabled people, *Disability and Society*, 9(1): 3–17.

Tisdall, E.K.M. (1996) Are young disabled people being sufficiently involved in their post school planning? Case studies of Scotland's future needs assessment and Ontario's educational–vocational meetings, *European Journal of Special Needs Education*, 11(1): 17–36.

UEA/NCB (University of East Anglia/National Children's Bureau) (2004) *Preliminary Report on the National Evaluation of Children's Trusts*. http//:www.everychildmatters.gov.uk/childrens-trusts/nationals-evaluation

Walker, A. (1982) *Unqualified and Underemployed: Handicapped People and the Labour Market*. London: National Children's Bureau.

Ward, K., Riddell, S., Dyer, M. and Thomson, G. (1991) *The Transition to Adulthood of Young People with Recorded Special Educational Needs*. Edinburgh: University of Edinburgh.

Warnock, M. (1978) *Report of the Committee of Enquiry into the Education of Handicapped Children and Young People*. London: Her Majesty's Stationery Office.

Weatherley, R.A. (1979) *Reforming Special Education: Policy Implementation from State Level to Street Level*. Cambridge, MA: MIT Press.

Wehmeyer, M., Agran, M. and Hughes, C. (1998) *Teaching Self Determination to Students with Disabilities*. Baltimore, MA: Paul H. Brookes.

Wertheimer, A. (ed.) (1995) *Circles of Support: Building Inclusive Communities*. Bristol: Circles Network.

Wilkinson, H. (2000) Caring, consuming and choosing, in S. Riddell and J. Salisbury (eds) *Gender, Policy and Educational Change: Shifting Agendas in the UK and Europe*. London: Routledge.

Willis, P. (1977) *Learning to Labour: How Working Class Kids Get Working Class Jobs*. Farnborough: Saxon House.

Wood, D. and Trickey, S. (1996) Transition planning: process or procedures, *British Journal of Special Education*, 23(3): 120–5.

Index

stimulation of aspiration 97
support in development of skills and
   capacities 97
support in making choices 98, 100
teaching approaches to support
   transition 100
transition-focused 95–100
underlying purpose 92
see also transition planning,
   improvement of

David Francis 13, 32, 49–50, 59, 61, 62,
   67–8
profile 110
social isolation, concerns over 60
decision making 28–43
   bureaucracy associated with process of
      4, 28
   choice and 29
   'choreography of decision making' 40
   complexity of 30, 42
   consensus decision making 31–2
   context relatedness 42
   decisions made but not enacted 37–8
   default decision making 39–40
   descriptive approaches to 28
   education continuation decisions 29
   'fate takes a hand' 33–4
   formality of procedures in 40–41
   incremental decisions or a leap in the
      dark 34–6
   individuals, relationships with systems
      and organizations 44–6
   information, importance of access to 41
   job placement decisions 29
   lone decision making 36–7
   normative approaches to 28
   patterns of processes of 30–31
   processes of 30–40
   professional-pupil relationship 46
   public process 41
   quasi-negotiated decisions 32–3
   range of types of 30
   residential placement decisions 29
   review meetings 41–2
   status, power and 41

support through understanding of 28
   see also policy framework
Department for Education and Science
   (DfES) 9
disability, social model of 63
Disability Discrimination Act (DDA)
   (1996) 26
Disability Equality Scheme 26, 99–100

ecosystemic theory (Bronfenbrenner) 44,
   46
Education Act (1993) 19
education policy 19–22
Education Reform Act (1988) 19
Education (Special Educational Needs)
   (England) Regulations (DfES, 2001)
   19
employment policy 23
Employment Service 23
*Enhancing Quality if Life: Facilitating
   Transitions for People with Profound and
   Complex Learning Difficulties* (Byers, et
   al. 2002) 43
Entry to Employment (E2E) scheme 23
European Agency for Development in
   Special Needs Education 10
Every Child Matters (DfES, 2003) 24–5, 26

family microsystem 44–5
14-19 Education and Skills White Paper
   (DfES, 2005) 22
Framework for Achievement 92
Further and Higher Education Act (1992)
   19, 20
Further Education Funding Council
   (FEFC) 20

Gavin Stone 13, 39, 46, 49–50, 60, 82, 85,
   103, 106
   aptitude lost in logistical considerations
      55
   parental support, lack of as influence on
      decision making 52–3
   profile 110

health and social care policy 23–4